CROSSROAD PRAYERS

AT GRADUATION AND OTHER VOCATIONAL WAYPOINTS

JESUS CALL,
YOUR CALL,
& NINETY DAYS OF PRAYER

Copyright © Robert Randoy
January 2019
All rights reserved.
ISBN: 9781795460606
Imprint: Independently published

Cover photo: ryoji-iwata – unsplash (royalty free)

Crossroad Prayers

DEDICATION

This little volume has emanated from years of prayers for our twelve amazing grandchildren, from their birth and childhood days, when we were blessed to have them living nearby, with many babysitting and family times together, and prayers also through their growing up years, with their families scattered all over North America.

Important for us all were and are their high school graduation days, and our efforts to be there with and for each one (often successful), with all our following prayers. The graduation crossroad, with those many and often difficult choices, especially vocational, is where this book of readings and prayers has come from.

We pray on for the ones now well past those grad days, and maybe facing new crossroads, for those still seeking but maybe not quite finding, and for those moving every day nearer the crossroad.

We pray all this for Christina and Kathryn; for David and Jennifer; for Caleb, Anya and Jonas; for Michael and Noa; and with special thanks for Chloe, Kalen and Hailey, for their shared thoughts and input for this book. Interwoven with these we pray thanksgiving for their parents, and for the blessing their prayers and their lives have been for each one.

It is with our family that all this began, but our prayers--and might we say also this dedication--reach much, much farther, toward every person who may take up this 90-day walk with the words of God, and the prayers.

Crossroad Prayers

CROSSROAD PRAYERS: INTRODUCTION

Grad Days, high school graduation: twelve years, and your last days and last hours together are running out. Grad Days, busy with many special events, moving steadily to the 'main event,' "the walk," the congratulations, the diploma.

Grad Days: are they a celebration, a satisfying completion of those years of study and labor, with maybe the taste of success? Or are they a celebration of being done with the study, and stresses of assignments and exams, a celebration of freedom?

Grad days: are they suddenly a time of memories, as you behold these familiar faces, classmates, and a life together, suddenly ending? Or have your school 'friending' experiences not been all that great? Probably something else has been looming over your grad days, that 'big question:' What's next? Where do I go from here? Graduation time is a *crossroads* time. Before you lie many roads, very different roads, more possibilities than you know. How do you know which road to take, which road is best for you?

The big question quickly breaks down into many smaller questions. What about a job? Is tomorrow the day to start looking? Where do I start?

Or maybe you have already started. Maybe it's exciting to think about earning a living, being on your own. Or maybe it's a little scary, that job search, knowing where to start, and putting together that resume that everyone says is so important. So many unknowns, so many decisions.

Another of the nearer, more immediate questions might be: what about more school? University? A trade school? A business school? An "IT" training program? Any of these might hold exciting possibilities. Many unknowns, many decisions.

Crossroad Prayers

Sometimes your friends or family may think they see your way quite clearly--and we all want good advice in dealing with many difficult choices--but you are the one who will weigh everything, and you are the one who will decide.

Of course, the whole process of job search, or program search is in itself a school, as you meet professionals in these areas, and learn to deal with people and new challenges, learn new skills, perhaps have tryouts, job experiences, or practicums. Maybe you have discovered that whatever you do, wherever you go, your path itself will become a school, and not an easy one.

Maybe Grad Days for you are about something more than a job, employment, or a paycheck. Maybe you have a dream or two, even from when you were little, something you really wanted to be "when you grew up." Maybe the dream hasn't gone away.

Rapper Kanye West came out with an album a few years ago. He titled it "Graduation," and his songs were not focused on classes and school life and diplomas, but about life questions and meanings, including one called "I Wonder."
Find your dreams come true
And I wonder if you know
What it means, what it means
And I wonder if you know
What it means to find your dreams
I've been waiting on this my whole life
These dreams be waking me up at night
You say I think I'm never wrong
You know what, maybe you're right
And I wonder if you know
What it means, what it means
And I wonder if you know
What it means to find your dreams

Crossroad Prayers

Is Grad Time for you about finding your dreams? What about finding your dreams in the excitement of a *career*?

"Career" is an interesting word. Dictionary definitions include words like 'profession' or 'occupation,' but the word literally means "a rush," and comes from a French word "*carrière,*" which means "a race course," and that word from the Latin "*carraria,*" which means "a wagon or carriage road". We are familiar of course with images and movies of vehicles "careering" or "careening" wildly, often out of control. Thinking, wondering, praying and following a career can lead to many good things, for yourself, and for others. But career making, rather than being a good, solid path toward a good goal, can also run wild, on bad roads, taking over a person's life, consuming it with being the 'greatest,' and riding the 'rich and famous' road, as we sadly hear of too often, with pop stars, for example, sometimes destroyed by the fame and the wealth.

Have you thought about a vocation? "*Vocation*" is also an interesting, and an important word. 'Vocation' can describe many jobs, trades or professions, but its root meaning is "a call, a summons." To have a call, or calling seems like something more than a job, or a career, because it suggests something outside yourself, something larger that is drawing, pulling, *calling* you.

I am thinking of a young girl, widely known now, a few years ago graduated from high school, who from early in her school years was strongly drawn to the importance and need of schools and education for young girls--this in a society that often denied these things to girls and to women. She blogged for the cause and was recognized beyond her home community. One day traveling in her school bus she was shot in the head by Taliban gunmen, with many others who were wounded or killed. After a difficult escape and a long recovery, she became known worldwide, because of her ongoing advocacy and a share in a Nobel Peace Prize(!), and through her book, "*I Am Malala*". Here is a young person with a calling.

Crossroad Prayers

Two others, young men from our part of the world also come to mind, as men with a calling that was much more than a job. One of them was Terry Fox, Canadian athlete and cancer research activist, who after being struck with cancer and the loss of a leg determined to run his *Marathon of Hope*, covering 5,373 kilometers, a full marathon each day, over 143 days, until the cancer took his life. Terry had a calling, a life calling, for his brief 22 years.

The other is Rick Hansen, victim of spinal cord injury at 15, which put him in a wheelchair, --and wheelchair athletics, Paralympics medals, and a lifelong labor for people with spinal cord injury and for public awareness and funds for research. Most notable was his *Man in Motion* world tour, 40,000 wheelchair kilometers in 34 countries around the world. A man with a calling.

We know many more stories, of old people and young people with a calling, most not so dramatic or widely known, but when you look closely, just as important and compelling, and amazing.

These pages however are about another calling, and another voice. You could say that this calling encompasses all the world's needs and crises, pains and suffering, and opportunities, because the voice that calls comes from another dimension, outside space and time--it comes from the presence of God! And yet at the same time the call is simple and down-to-earth, because the one calling is also a human being, a man, one who is like us and who knows us. He knows you and where you came from and where you are going, and he has already been there. I think you know who he is, and that his name is Jesus Christ. His impossible and simple call is "Follow me."

"While walking by the Sea of Galilee, (Jesus) saw two brothers, Simon (who is called Peter) and Andrew his brother, casting a net into the sea, for they were fishermen. And he said to them, 'Follow me, and I will make you fishers of men.' Immediately they left their nets and followed him. And going on from there he saw two other brothers, James the son of Zebedee and John his brother, in the boat with

Crossroad Prayers

Zebedee their father, mending their nets, and he called them. Immediately they left the boat and their father and followed him." (Matthew 4:18-22, ESV throughout) Simple and down-to-earth as could be, yet the longer you look and the better you listen, the better you can hear and see how Jesus' call to follow does touch and also encompass all the world's needs and possibilities. "Follow me" is simple, yet with Jesus you might go anywhere.

So facing Grad time we should know that this is not the only crossroad, where you will decide where your life should be headed. Many who study the workplace and our economy and demographics tell us that very few people will find themselves in any lifelong work; rather most will work in a number of different positions and workplaces over their working years. Maybe you have passed your ten year high school reunion, or twenty years. Still at every crossroad it is always Jesus' voice and call you want to hear. His call has everything to do with whatever job, career, trade, profession or life-work that you could ever think about, or wrestle with. And Jesus is the first one to whom you want to bring your questions because he knows you, and all the roads you might follow, and he knows the best possible road for you. These questions become your prayers, and your prayers are what these next pages are about.

Crossroad Prayers

THE BRICK

The bricklayer laid a brick on the bed of cement.
Then, with a precise stroke of his trowel spread another layer
And without a by-your-leave, laid on another brick.
The foundations grew visibly,
The building rose, tall and strong, to shelter men.

I thought, Lord, of that brick buried in the darkness at the base of the big building.
No one sees it, but it accomplishes its task, and the other bricks need it.
Lord, what difference whether I am on the roof-top or in the foundations of your building, as long as I stand faithfully in the right place?

THERE ARE TWO LOVES ONLY

There are two loves only, Lord,
Love of myself and love of you and of others…

Grant me, Lord, to spread true love in the world.
Grant that by me and by your children it may penetrate a little
    into all circles, all societies, all economic and political systems,
        all laws, all contracts, all rulings;
Grant that it may penetrate into offices, factories, apartment buildings. cinemas, dance-halls;
Grant that it may penetrate the hearts of men and that I may never forget that the battle
for a better world is a battle of love, in the service of love.

Help me to love, Lord,…

By Michel Quoist, *Prayers of life* (Dublin, Gill and MacMillan, 1966)

Table of Contents

DEDICATION ii
CROSSROAD PRAYERS: INTRODUCTION iii
THE BRICK viii
THERE ARE TWO LOVES ONLY viii
DAY 1. ONE ROAD TO ANYWHERE 1
DAY 2. WHAT IS THE WAY? WHO IS THE WAY? 3
DAY 3. THE HARD WAY, THE BEAUTIFUL WAY 4
Day 4. LOSING AND FINDING 6
DAY 5. LIFE TOGETHER--ON THE JOB 7
DAY 6. THE SERVANT 9
DAY 7. FOOT WASHING IS GOOD 11
DAY 8. JESUS AT YOUR JOBSITE 13
DAY 9. LEVI AND YOU 15
DAY 10. GET REAL; OUR WORLD IS BROKEN 17
DAY 11. DOMINION 19
DAY 12. SCIENCE IN GENESIS ONE 21
DAY 13. MALE AND FEMALE 23
DAY 14. FEMALE, MALE AND WORK 25
DAY 15. YES OR NO 27
DAY 16. WARTIME PRAYERS 29
DAY 17. WORK IS GOOD 31
DAY 18. WORK AS WORSHIP 32
DAY 19. BROTHERS, SISTERS, KEEPERS 34
DAY 20. ADAM'S TV 36
DAY 21. WHEN YOUR NAME IS CALLED 38
DAY 22. IMMANUEL AND YOUR WORKPLACE 39
DAY 23. PERFECT WORD 41

DAY 24. GOD'S HONOR	43
DAY 25. GOD'S GLORY, NOT THE WORLD'S	45
DAY 26. LIBERATION CALL	47
DAY 27. HAPPY CONFESSION	49
DAY 28. UNLOCKING PRISONS	51
DAY 29. LIKE ROCKY	53
DAY 30. HE KNOWS YOU	55
DAY 31. ENERGIZED BY WORK?	57
DAY 32. LOVE SHAKING THE WORLD	59
Day 33. THE GOOD NEWS--HOWEVER	61
DAY 34. WORK AND WORSHIP	63
DAY 35. MORE ON THE WILD SIDE	65
DAY 36. ONE OF A KIND	67
DAY 37. CARDIO CHECK	69
DAY 38. A PROPHET?	71
DAY 39. SERVANT	73
DAY 40. TEACHER!	74
DAY 41. ENCOURAGERS!	76
DAY 42. GIVERS LIFESTYLE	78
DAY 43. SERVANT LEADER	79
DAY 44. ARMY OF MERCY	80
DAY 45. SMALL AND IRREPLACEABLE	82
DAY 46. NOW YOU DO IT	84
DAY 47. JESUS' FAMILY BUSINESS	86
DAY 48. THE HEALER	88
DAY 49. RAISE THE DEAD	90
DAY 50. INTO COMMUNITY	92
DAY 51. DEMONS DOWN	94

DAY 52. JESUS' CROSSROAD PRAYERS	96
DAY 53. FATHER	97
DAY 54. HOW GOOD CAN IT GET?	99
DAY 55. DISCIPLES' PRAYER	101
DAY 56. YOUR HOLY NAME	103
DAY 57. GOD RULES!	105
DAY 58. THE GOOD WILL	107
DAY 59. BREAD IS A BIG WORD	108
DAY 60. OUR FOOD AND CLOTHING	110
DAY 61. OUR HOME AND PROPERTY	112
DAY 62. OUR WORK AND INCOME	114
DAY 63. DEVOTED FAMILY	116
DAY 64. GOD'S HEART FOR THE BROKEN	118
DAY 65. WHO HEARS THE CRY?	120
DAY 66. FAVOURABLE WEATHER!	122
DAY 67. DEEP PEACE	124
DAY 68. PEACEMAKERS	126
DAY 69. A GOOD NAME	128
DAY 70. THE CORPORATION	130
DAY 71. BREATH OF LIFE	132
DAY 72. WARTIME PRAYER	134
DAY 73. WARTIME PRAYER-- CONTINUED	136
DAY 74. WORK AND PRAISE	138
DAY 75. JESUS' PRAYER FOR YOU	140
DAY 76. JESUS' ONE BODY	141
DAY 77. GLORY	143
DAY 78. THE ROAD FOR YOU	145
DAY 79. BAPTIZING AND TEACHING	147

DAY 80. FIND THE WAY TOGETHER	149
DAY 81. ALL YOU NEED AND MORE	151
DAY 82. JESUS IN THE WORKPLACE	153
DAY 83. YOUR WAR ZONE	155
DAY 84. ENEMY DOWN	157
DAY 85. TEN FIGHTING WORDS	159
DAY 86. FAMILY WARZONE/WORKPLACE?	161
DAY 87. LIFE IN THE SHADOW OF DEATH	163
DAY 88. GOD'S ECONOMY	164
DAY 89. LIFE WORD	166
DAY 90. WEAPONS OR TOOLS	168
ACKNOWLEDGEMENTS	170
ABOUT THE AUTHOR	171

DAY 1. ONE ROAD TO ANYWHERE

Matthew 7:13-14; Psalm 16:11

Smartphones, computer, internet: one global electronic road for everyone to travel, but it goes anywhere, everywhere on earth, quickly, easily and maybe even to places you don't want to be. Learning the road can be complicated and challenging, but unless we want to hide ourselves away we need to learn this electronic road as best we can.

Jesus' call to follow him is something like that. It is one road, his road, but he might take you anywhere. The big difference with his road, of course, is that he knows the best, the right places for you to go, to live, to work, and he knows those places that anyone in their right mind would never want to go, or live or work.

The 'e-world' has many ports of entry, but you want the right one and your efforts will be worthless if you miss it. So Jesus said about his road, his way and port of entry: "Enter by the narrow gate, for the gate is wide and the way is easy that leads to destruction, and those who enter by it are many. For the gate is narrow and the way is hard that leads to life, and those who find it are few." (Matt.7; 13f)

Is it hard to see what Jesus' word means for you if you are searching not only for a life, but at this crossroad also for a lifework, a job, a career, whatever you want to call it? Jesus' gate and pathway have to do with all of life, every day, every breath, and therefore most certainly and importantly with your crossroad/workplace decisions.

Most importantly Jesus wants, more than we do, that we find the narrow gate and the hard way that leads to a full life, as he said often, in different ways, "I came that they may have life and have it abundantly." (Jn. 10:10) This word is for all your life, and in a special way for your job or career path. This word in essence is about life with him, life with God, life walking close to him who knows the way.

Crossroad Prayers

Lord, finding my way in life, at this crossroad, is difficult, so much is hard to see and hard to understand. Show me how important my work life is in my whole life as your follower. Amen

DAY 2. WHAT IS THE WAY?   WHO IS THE WAY?
John 14:1-7

So many roads, so many workplaces, jobs, careers, vocations, those you have thought about, those others have told you about, and how many surprises might show up?

But from the start Jesus calls us to one road only, exactly the same road for every follower. That road may take you anywhere, and it will take his followers to many different places, but it is always the same road, and you can't really draw it on a map.

Jesus' disciple Thomas was frustrated with what Jesus was saying about the very last stage of the way, the indescribable, unimaginable end of the road, "In my Father's house." Thomas complained, "Lord, we don't know where you are going. How can we know the way?" (Jn 14:5) Jesus said to him much the same thing he had said from the beginning, if not in the same words: *"I am the way"* (and the truth and the life also) "No one can come to the Father except through me."

Very simple, even though his words are more than we can fathom, but that's alright. Jesus knows what he is doing and where he is taking us.´ Here it is, the one and only road, which is taking us who knows where? He knows where and he is calling us to follow, day by every day. This is our life as disciples; it is your life, and it is your life work, all at the same time.

Jesus is the way and he is the truth, and as the truth he shows you the truth of who you are, and what your life can be, and what your life work can be, not only in the particulars, but also in its fullness.

   Thank you Lord, it all seems so simple and clear, yet sometimes I can't understand it at all. I need to find where to go from this crossroad. Thank you for offering yourself as the way; help me to stick close to you, whatever. Thank you

DAY 3. THE HARD WAY, THE BEAUTIFUL WAY
Mark 1:14-15; Isaiah 45:22

What is the first thing we need to know about Jesus' way, his hard and life-giving way? And what does it all have to do with a job, a profession, a life work?

"Now after John was arrested, Jesus came into Galilee, proclaiming the Gospel of God, and saying, 'The time is fulfilled, and the kingdom of God is at hand; repent and believe in the Gospel." (Mk. 1:14)

You turn on your phone, touch the screen, pick your program or app, and send your message; you're on your way. We probably don't think of it often, how amazing it is and how simple.

Jesus' way, his narrow gate is in a way very simple; it is there in Mark's words, six words; "Repent and believe the gospel." But at the same time it is the hardest thing a human being ever does. It is the hardest thing in life to make that 180 degree turnaround from the centre of mind and heart, that complete turn-- away from myself and from everything that comes naturally and easily, and toward Jesus, toward God, toward life. Toward that way of believing him, trusting Him, counting, depending on him totally in everything I think or say or do.

This is what "follow me" means, not just that first time, but all the time and every day.

So as you stand at this life-call crossroad, here is the first step in all your choices, and all the choices that follow, in all the years ahead.

Turning away from myself and toward Jesus is about a *relationship* with him, and with his Father. In this relationship He is with you every day and in every choice, including whether or not you should apply for that job you just heard about, and may look promising, or that university degree and that profession. Jesus has no "distance plan" for information or education or advice. His plan is *himself*, his presence; and prayer his connection. It is never easy, but it grows steadily, day by day; it is life, his life in our life, our life in his life, and the only life.

Saying no to myself and yes to Jesus does not mean turning away from or rejecting the possibilities, the opportunities that most interest or excite me. It does mean that, following him, I am much better able to find them.

Lord, help me reflect on what my repentance/turnaround means. Help me understand how hard it is, but also how good it is to be with you on your way as my way. Can you teach me the 'joy of repentance,' even also the joy of turning away from a not-so-good workplace and toward a much better one? Amen

Crossroad Prayers

Day 4. LOSING AND FINDING

Matthew 16:24-26

So here I stand at my crossroad, and maybe my mind is swimming with the job or career possibilities before me. So how does Jesus' life-call to repent and to trust him help me find my way? How does saying *no* to self and *yes* to him show me the way? It doesn't seem to make sense. Yet Jesus says it, again and again.

"For whoever would save his life will lose it, but whoever loses his life for my sake will find it." (Matt. 6:25)

Losing is finding. Losing, giving up the self-centred way, abandoning the natural, easy way. and simply following, trusting Jesus, whatever he says, is finding oneself, finding our own true life, and --can we say it?--the life we were meant for. Following him is finding your *whole* life, including the work life you puzzle over and struggle with.

Everyone wants to have "the good life," whatever that means; everyone also wants to have a work life, a job, a career that in some way is a good life. Those who lose their life to find it, following Jesus, discover that good life, which the Psalmist sang about: "In the way of your testimonies I delight as much as in all riches." (Ps.119:14)

The Psalmist had learned that God's word and lifestyle are in themselves better than any paycheck we may earn.   "The law of your mouth is better to me than thousands of gold and silver pieces." (Psalm 119:72 "Your testimonies are my delight; they are my counselors." (V. 24)
In all your searching it is Jesus himself who will be your counselor. His call to you at your crossroad is to a life way, a life work that is your delight.

LORD, you know I would really like to have a work life that is a joy and a delight. Is is actually possible? For me? Help me take you at your word that losing myself to you is finding myself and my way. Thank you

Crossroad Prayers

DAY 5. LIFE TOGETHER--ON THE JOB

Mark 12:28-34

The 'losing yourself' part of Jesus' call is always the hard part, but the 'finding yourself' and finding his way for you is that Psalmist's joy and delight, and it is meant to be ours. Jesus shows his followers quite clearly how and why it is joy and delight and how it brings us to life. He showed this beautifully one day when he was questioned about which of all the commandments was the greatest. He said, "You shall love the Lord your God with all your heart and with all your soul, and with all your mind. This is the first and greatest commandment. And a second is like it: you shall love your neighbor as yourself." (Matt.22:35ff)

Finding the good life is following Jesus and learning to love God with everything we have and everything we are and at the same time learning how to love the people in our world—including ourselves. Learning to love ourselves may sometimes seem the hardest part. Here Jesus shows us the good life, and this life is about *love relationships,* first and most with our God, and inseparably, with people.

So your question of course is: what does Jesus' word here mean for you at your crossroad, as you try to find your way to a good life, a good work life? It means this--that your life, also your job, your career, is not about *things*, whether money, or personal achievements, or any other things. Your work life also is about relationships, loving God and loving people.

You have already realized in the push and pull of the jobs you have had how important relationships are, and how, for example in the business world, the hardest part of the workday is people, coworkers, managers, just getting along with each other, without getting caught up in competitions, personal irritations, or personality conflicts. Jesus' followers are of course called to something more and better than just 'getting along.' We are called to honour and love him wholly in everything we do, also in loving the people around us--here the people we work with. His followers will more than 'make a difference;' they will

Crossroad Prayers

be his own blessing on that workplace, whatever the business or profession.

Lord, you know how I relate to people, how I get along. You know where I can do well and where I have problems. Help me stay close, so I can know and love you better, and so That your love can spill over onto the people I live and work with.

DAY 6. THE SERVANT

Mark 10:35-45

Think about your job search, your life-work, and then about how hard it can sometimes be to work well together with others. Jesus and his disciples were a working group, as he taught them and trained them in their calling. And they had a problem. That day it started with brothers James and John, with their desire for a kind of future promotion. They asked him, "Grant us to sit, one at your right hand and one at your left, in your glory." (Mk.10:37)

Jesus asked them some hard questions before explaining that such an appointment wasn't in his job description. But as soon as their co-workers heard of all this, they of course "began to be indignant at James and John." (v.41)

Does this feel like a familiar workplace problem?

It was Jesus' perfect teaching opportunity to turn them back again to the way of life, and away from the self-serving way, the wide and easy way, the world's way. "You know that those who are considered rulers of the Gentiles lord it over them, and their great ones exercise authority over them, But *it shall not be so among you.*" (v.42) Then Jesus showed them and demonstrated his basic job description, and theirs.

"But whoever would be great among you must be your servant, and whoever would be first among you must be slave of all." Then the clincher: "For even the Son of Man came not to be served, but to serve, and to give his life as a ransom for many." (v423ff)

Here in the most practical terms we learn how to lose one's self to find one's self. Here is following Jesus the servant by learning to be servants. He served perfectly and amazingly, and always. And we are in his school, learning the primary lesson, little by little, day by day.

Crossroad Prayers

So it doesn't matter what your work, career, or profession; if you are following Jesus' call you are learning to be a servant in that place, that job, that work. And how your work world needs you, and is looking for you.

Lord, I like being served better than being a servant, and I need your help, a lot of help. So help me live and walk very close to you, so I can learn the servant way. Amen

DAY 7. FOOT WASHING IS GOOD
John 13:1-17

The one who wants to be greatest, to be first, must be a servant, a free and willing, even happy slave, or bondservant (Jesus' chosen term)! Actually, our whole society knows down deep that *serving* is what life and work are meant to be. We use the servant language all the time. We speak of government workers, for example, as "public servants." We speak of business and retail as service, checkout counters as "service centres," and everybody in the shops and supermarkets are always saying that "we are here to serve."

As always, it is much easier to talk service than to do it, and easier to look like a servant than to be one. It is so much easier to work for ourselves than to seriously sign up for Jesus' servant school.

Jesus brought all this very much down-to-earth on the night he was betrayed, when he "Rose from supper... and laid aside his outer garments, and taking a towel, tied it around his waist. Then he poured water into a basin and began to wash the disciples' feet and to wipe them with the towel…" (John 13:4ff)

This was a difficult experience for his followers, both in letting Jesus wash their feet, and certainly also to receive his teaching of the servant life. "Do you understand what I have done to you? You call me teacher and Lord, and you are right, for so I am. If I then, your Lord and teacher, have washed your feet, you also ought to wash one another's feet. For I have given you an example, that you also should do just as I have done to you." (John 13:13ff)

Foot washing is not part of our 21st century daily routine, but we have all kinds of practical, down-to-earth opportunities to help one another with household, personal or neighbourly needs, and to practice our new servant life and skills, and exercise our 'new servant heart.'

Crossroad Prayers

Again, this everyday servant life means also your work life, job, profession, and belongs in all your crossroad prayers. How does Jesus' servant call affect your search? Does it throw any new light? In what kind of work might you, with your own uniqueness and gifts, best be a servant to him and to the people around you?

Thank you, Lord for that foot washing night with your twelve. And thank you for all the times and ways that you have washed my feet. Thank you also for showing me how good it is to forget myself and bless somebody else with an everyday need, also at work. Amen

Crossroad Prayers

DAY 8. JESUS AT YOUR JOBSITE
Luke 5:1-11

The day when you went to that office or restaurant to interview for a job, or to start work, did Jesus show up? Maybe you prayed he would be with you in meeting the personnel manager or the boss, and maybe he was.

Jesus met his first disciples at least once at their jobsite. Actually, he was doing his own teaching work right next to Simon Peter's fishing boat on the Gennesaret lakeshore, while Simon and partners were washing their nets. Then, probably with a smile, Jesus "commandeered" one of the boats, "And he sat down and taught the people from the boat."

That might have been it, and he might have just thanked Simon and gone his way. But Jesus had much more in mind, so he puzzled these fishermen with a bit of unprofessional advice: "Put out into the deep and let down your nets for a catch." (Luke 5:3f) Simon answered, "Master, we toiled all night and took nothing. But at your word I will let down the nets." (v5) What happened next shook them all, Simon onto his knees.

The nets quickly "enclosed a large number of fish and their nets were breaking." Their partners were signaled to "come and help them. And they came and filled both the boats, so that they began to sink." (v.6f)

Jesus met these men at their workplace and told them where to put their nets. Why? So that they could realize who he was. So Simon went to his knees, and said, "Depart from me O Lord." But Jesus only drew him closer, and there gave Simon his calling. "Do not be afraid, for now you will be catching **people**. And when they had brought their boats to land, they left everything and followed him." (v.11) Jesus met Simon and Andrew, James and John at their workplace so that he could call them to a greater work.

As we show up for a job or an interview, even with Jesus present, in our heart, our mind, our prayers, we probably don't expect some sign or

Crossroad Prayers

wonder, like that boatload of fish, but he wants us to hear again his call to work with him, whatever the jobsite. One more thing: Simon's work would not be for fish, but for people. So with his call to you, on that construction site, or the fast food place, or the medical lab. It is always about people, and serving.

Lord, I would like to envision you, present at my workplace, and even though I don't know what You would say or do, I want to trust that you would be in and with me, with us, whatever we are doing. Amen

DAY 9. LEVI AND YOU
Luke 5:27-32

Jesus showed up another day at the workplace of another who became a follower. "After this (Jesus) went out and saw a tax collector named Levi, sitting at the tax booth. and he said to him, 'Follow me." And leaving everything, he rose and followed him." (Luke 5:22f)

Most people, then and now, are inclined to have no more to do with tax people than necessary; but Jesus' fellow Jews avoided the whole company of their tax collectors, who were mostly collaborators with the Roman occupiers and unregulated profiteers as well.

But Jesus quite deliberately stops at Levi's (Matthew's) shop, here again mixing with the wrong kind of people. When Jesus said, "Follow me" Levi in that moment saw everything in a new light and abandoned his old life, his old work and followed. Whatever he had seen or heard from or about Jesus before this, Levi knew Jesus and his way was what he wanted. He didn't know where Jesus would lead, but he did know he didn't want anything less or anything else. Here we have Levi, losing himself and finding himself.

Another day, another meeting, another tax collector, actually a "chief of tax collectors and rich." (Lk.19:2) Here of course it was that little man who climbed a tree to see Jesus. Zacchaeus it was who had heard much about him. Right away Jesus invited himself to Zacchaeus' fancy home, once more to hang out with the wrong crowd. But this time Jesus did not call the tax collector to quit his job, rather he called and celebrated a tax man who suddenly and totally changed his ways. Zacchaeus said to Jesus, "Behold, Lord; the half of my goods I give to the poor. And if I have defrauded anyone of anything, I restore it fourfold." (Luke 19:8)

These are the kind of things that can happen at any workplace where Jesus shows up.

Crossroad Prayers

Thank you Lord for Levi and Zacchaeus and what your presence means, also for our own world and its ways of greed, theft and corruption. Lord, what would it mean if you called me to be your presence in some government position? Amen

DAY 10. GET REAL; OUR WORLD IS BROKEN
Mark 2:13-17

Searching for a job, a career, a life work is never going to be easy, a smooth road or trouble free. Your school years weren't and your crossroad search won't be, and the main reason is because we are live in a very broken world.

This is the world we see at Levi's party, the one he gave at his house after he made his big move and became Jesus' disciple. 'As he reclined at table in his house, many tax collectors and sinners were reclining with Jesus and his disciples...." (Mark 2:15)

Levi and his old friends, and his new friends. The religious leaders were always watching Jesus' irresponsible and bad behavior and complained to some disciples, "Why does he eat with tax collectors and sinners?" (v.16)

Jesus heard and saw again how they just didn't get it. They could not or would not see that they along with everyone else were part of this very broken world, broken most of all at the heart and centre of life. So he said, "Those who are well have no need of a physician, but those who are sick. I came not to call the righteous, but sinners." (2:17)

These important people, religious leaders, were all just as much in need of a doctor for the heart, the mind, the spirit, as were Levi's crowd of sinners, and all the rest of us. So whatever road you take from today's crossroad will be a challenge, and difficult. But with Jesus at the junction and the workplace you can be totally realistic, and not be thrown by the problems of human beings, working or not working together, or workplace politics, or the dead-end trails. You walk through it all together with the only physician who can deal with all the brokenness and also lead us into healing and wholeness. "And great crowds came to him, bringing with them the lame, the blind, the crippled, the mute, and many others, and they put them at his feet, and He healed them." (Matthew 15:30)

Crossroad Prayers

Lord, it is hard to know how to handle the problems and obstacles which seem so often unnecessary. Help me make allowances for people and our world's brokenness--which does include me. Help me follow you, stay close every step, every day, and remember to thank you for your healing, mending work. Thank you for your great rehab plan for us all as followers. Amen

DAY 11. DOMINION

Genesis 1:1-26

As you think about your crossroad and which is the best road you can follow, and as you reflect on the brokenness of our world and human life, it is important to try a little time travel, back to the time before time, or before the years can be numbered, way back even before the great human breakdown happened, the crash, or as it is usually called, "the Fall."

In all we know of the days of beginnings, God created and called our first parents, and wonderfully blessed them with his whole new world as their *workplace*. God created light and water and the heavens; he created vegetation, plants and trees, and sea creatures and birds and "and every creature that moved." "Then God said 'Let us make man in our image, after our likeness. And let them have dominion over the fish of the sea and over the birds of the heavens and over the livestock and over all the earth." (Genesis 1:26)

God the creator is the natural and perfect Lord over everything he made. But in those first and early days God gives humans **dominion**, or a lordship over the whole of his earthly creation. The whole earth is given as our workplace, to learn everything about it, and to manage it--in God's good way, as people made in God's very image.

What greater work could anyone imagine? To begin to realize what God has called us to should take our breath away. And to reflect on what dominion means opens to us all the human sciences and arts, all there is to be learned and all the good that can be done with all we learn.

This probably doesn't help you to narrow your search or your choices, but it surely opens up endless possibilities, which is important too.

"When I look at your heavens, the work of your fingers,
The moon and the stars, which you have set in place,
What is man, that you are mindful of him,

Crossroad Prayers

and the son of man, that you care for him?
Yet you have made him a little lower than the heavenly beings
And crowned him with glory and honor.
You have given him dominion over the works of your hands…" (Psalm 8:3ff)

Shall I look for a while at your heavens and the earth which you have put into our human hands? What does dominion really mean for us, for me today? And to what part of this dominion, to what kind of work are you calling me?

DAY 12. SCIENCE IN GENESIS ONE
Psalm 139:13-17

In your school years chemistry, physics, biology courses did you ever experience the excitement of discovery in learning how our world and our bodies are put together? Have you wondered what a career in scientific research would be like? Much research was surely included in God's first call to our first parents: "Now out of the ground the Lord God had formed every beast of the field and every bird of the heavens and brought them to the man to see what he would call them. And whatever the man called every living creature, that was its name." (Genesis 2:19)

This same work God blessed Adam with is in no way finished. Today's ongoing science every day leads to ongoing 'namings.' I am amazed at the sciences of cellular biology, particularly of the past century, which led to the discovery of the microscopic "factories," the tens of trillions of cells that make up our bodies, and the naming of the component parts, the *organelles*, like *mitochondria, ribosomes, centromeres*, and many more. God's call to examine and to name everything has not been finished or cancelled.

God's earliest days/first **call** to human beings was into this science workplace, to learn how our world and our bodies are put together and how they function, and becomes ever more important in our generations, living as we do with all these centuries of breakdown of life and health in our 'fallen' world. How many suffering people everywhere are looking and waiting for the medical sciences' chemical and biological help with our diseases and the cell damage we all live with?

Many have heard Jesus' call to follow him as aides to the great physician, in this work of searching, seeking, and discovery. Maybe you are hearing it.

Something more and even better comes with Jesus' call to science and research (and in every other work); that *more* is the joy of praise and thanksgiving. It is what the Psalmist found in his learning, in his living and his self-examination: "I praise you, for I am fearfully and wonderfully made. Wonderful are your works; my soul knows it very well." (Psalm 139:14)

Lord, help me to pay attention to my own body and how wonderfully I am made, so that I can thank you, so that I can take good care of myself, and so that I can serve and bless, in life and in health, the people in my world. Amen

DAY 13. MALE AND FEMALE

Genesis 2:15-25

Here I am at my crossroad; where am I going, what is the very best road for me to take? Or is there another question that should come first: Who am I? Learning to know myself as well as I can must come before I can find my way in life and work. Well, here God may surprise you as he points to yet another road to consider: your identity as man or woman.

"So God created man in his own image, in the image of God he created him, *male and female* he created them." And God blessed them. And God said to them, 'Be fruitful and multiply, and fill the earth... ('and have dominion...') (Genesis 1:27f)

How is that for a call from God for your life? And how does it fit with your crossroad search for work life or a life work? It may strike you as a huge complication, maybe more than you want to deal with. But there it is. God declared it, and it isn't going to go away. You know anyway that the male and female is always somewhere in your mind, emotions and longings? Many thoughts have come to mind, about boyfriends, girlfriends you have known--or not; maybe thoughts of marriage, thoughts of family, and what all this means for your work life questions.

Ready or not, God's word here does throw another light on your crossroads search, even if you see no answer right now. Many complications, possible problems may come to mind, with no easy answers or resolutions, but only God's clear and strong vision of a rich and good life, with his great blessing in 'being fruitful and multiplying,' along with 'having dominion over the earth,' all of it somehow together. Here most important to know and remember is that when God calls us he will always show the way, for each and all of his unique and gifted servants.

Thank you Lord that you know all my thoughts and desires, good and not so good, in being female or male, and you know my problems, my

Crossroad Prayers

struggles and sometimes confusion. You know how it all is supposed to fit together, as I try to find where to go from this crossroad. Show me my way. Amen

DAY 14. FEMALE, MALE AND WORK

Genesis 2:15-25

Every person standing at a graduation or other crossroad has long struggled with who she or he is, with becoming a woman, becoming a man, and where to proceed on that pathway.

Many, however, have not caught the beauty and the joy of God's call. God gave the woman to the man and she was his delight. We also must know that the man was the woman's delight. "The man said, 'This at last is bone of my bones, and flesh of my flesh; she shall be called woman, because she was taken out of man.'" (Gen.2:23)

Much more should be said about the whole of the story, but we need to see the joy; 'Therefore a man shall leave his father and his mother and hold fast to his wife, and they shall become one flesh." (Gen.2:24)

We also can sense their delight, and the peace and freedom of this life in intimate relationship with God and with each other. "And the man and his wife were both naked and were not ashamed." (v.25) Again God reminds us that life is not about things or ideas or money; life is about relationship with God and with each other. It is about loving God with all we have and loving each other, wife or husband first. In marriage is God's starting place for all human relationships.

The Netflix series on the *Crown*, which told the story of Britain's royal family and palace staff, and the government, especially Prime Ministers and Cabinet, seemed to be mostly the story of troubled marriages and troubled lives, especially in many 'work problems' of leaders of state and of government which were created by marriage problems.

Whatever God can give and teach of his plan for us as male and female, his gift and path for marriage may more than anything else shape our life work and calling. Our joy and satisfaction will come with our receiving and learning his gift; our pain and sorrow and trouble will come with not receiving, never learning.

Crossroad Prayers

Difficult and complicated though it may be, God's call to us as female and male can't be separated from his call to our work.

God also calls his people to singleness. This call is also good and also fruitful in many, many ways. God called Jesus to singleness. The oneness of love belongs to singleness, too; in how many and wonderful ways, God knows, and shows.

Lord, both your callings upon me are way more than I can manage. Just show me what I need to learn today. Amen

DAY 15. YES OR NO

Genesis 3:1-7

First God calls, then the person called considers it, and whether to say yes... or no. Adam listened when God called him to his work, to have dominion, and said yes. "The man gave names to all livestock and to the birds of the heavens, and to every beast of the field." (Gen. 2:20)

He said yes also to the woman God gave. But one day their yes became no, and all life on earth changed for all time. It happened when an alien voice was heard in that garden, the voice of 'the serpent.' The voice began a conversation, first with a question for the woman: "Did God actually say, 'You shall not eat of any tree of the garden?'" (Gen. 3:1) Just a simple question with a little truth in it.

So the woman answered, "We may eat of the fruit of the trees in the garden, but God said, 'You shall not eat of the fruit of the tree in the midst of the garden, neither shall you touch it, lest you die.'" (vv 2,3)

Next came the serpent's denial: "You will not surely die." God is lying, says the father of lies. And denial becomes accusation: "God knows that when you eat of it your eyes will be opened and you will be like God, knowing good and evil." (vv.4,5) God is only serving himself, the voice says, protecting his interests, denying you his knowledge and your right to be like him.

Too much for them it was: "So when the woman saw that the tree was good for food, and that it was a delight to the eyes, and that the tree was to be desired to make one wise, she took of the fruit and ate, and she also gave some to her husband, and he ate." (v.6)

In this moment their lives became **no** to God, an unholy turning, away from God and into themselves; a new serving, not God, not each other, but each for the self. And so our world has been until today, and will be until God calls everything to its end. A self-serving world can never work, even for two people, let alone our billions.

Crossroad Prayers

As you pray God to show you your own workplace pathway, his calling for you in this our world of **no**--with all its hurt and need and brokenness, think of that ancient moment when our first parents could have said yes to their God, but did not. And thank him that today you can say yes to his good word and to his call.

Lord, help me hear you clearly, help me recognize the liar's voice, and help me to freely and happily offer you my unqualified yes. Amen

DAY 16. WARTIME PRAYERS

Genesis 3:8-15

Our world of "no," in which we live and the world in which we pray God to show us our calling, our life work, is a world at war. This is inevitable of course if every human being is by nature living and working to serve himself, herself, and not God or one another. Wartime is a given. Our wartime is not always violent or bloody, but it is where we live.

Every business or university, every corporation or industry is run by men and women who are usually competing with each other for position, power or money. Underneath the nice words and smiles--God love them all--it is wartime.

When God asked our first parents, "Have you eaten of the tree of which I commanded you not to eat?" The man blamed the woman, and the woman blamed the serpent. And God spoke of the wartime world which was to come and which we wake up to every morning. God spoke first a curse on the serpent, and God told what life on earth would be like until the end. "I will put enmity between you and the woman, and between your offspring and her offspring; he shall bruise your head, and you shall bruise his heel." (Gen.3:15)

This enmity means ongoing war between Eve's children, every generation, and all those Voices like the serpent's voice, always denying whatever God has said, and accusing Him of being the enemy.

Whatever work world Jesus may send you into, never be surprised at the conflicts, at people against each other, competing for position, power, money, and often dysfunctional workplaces. No surprises at some bruises in the process either. It's a world of accusation and blame. But your prayers, your persistence in following Jesus, will not only bring you through, but will also, day by day bring ruin to the enemy's work--until that day when God finally 'crushes his head.'

Crossroad Prayers

Lord I don't always remember, or even realize that our world is at war, and I don't know what it all means for my work, my calling. But thank you, that you see it all and that you are able to prepare me for anything. Amen

DAY 17. WORK IS GOOD

Genesis 3:16-21

In our crossroads praying we naturally have in mind a kind of work we can enjoy, with pleasant working conditions, even though we can remember God's early warning and difficult promise that it won't be easy. To Adam he said, "Cursed is the ground because of you; in pain you shall eat of it all the days of your life." He spoke of the "thorns and thistles," and "By the sweat of your brow you shall eat bread."

So it is that most of us speak of TGIF, and the work-week's end, and 'Monday morning blues." So it is, all because they ate of the tree, against God's command, all because they said "no" to God and headed out on that bad road, that "**no**" way of life.

But remember that God cursed the serpent, but not Adam, not Eve, not even the ground. The rebellion cursed the ground. Most important, all the curses did not negate God's *first call,* or the reality that the work God gave was the same good gift and blessing it was in the beginning. It still is. His call and his promise we remember: "Be fruitful and multiply and fill the earth and subdue it, and have dominion" over the fish, the birds and every living thing. "And God saw everything that He had made, and behold, it was very good." (Gen. 1:31)

Even after the 'fall' and the resulting curse, the work given remained and remains very good, and we help each other remember this as we pray our crossroad prayers, and seek the road and the workplace to which Jesus sends us

Lord, when I don't feel like getting up and going to work, or write up and send out resumes or applications, remind me, and teach me, more and better, how very good was the work you gave to our first parents, and how good is the work you give to me, in itself, and not just because of the paycheck. Amen

Crossroad Prayers

DAY 18. WORK AS WORSHIP

Adam and Eve through all the struggle and the pain of their *no* to God, did turn back, they repented and began to follow him, and began to learn the difficult *"yes, Lord"* way of life. So: "Adam knew Eve his wife, and she conceived and bore Cain, saying, 'I have gotten a man with the help of the Lord.' And again, she bore his brother, Abel." (Gen. 4:1f)

Just as God had said: "Be fruitful and multiply." The very next thing we read in Genesis 4 is about the work these brothers were called to. We know nothing of any 'crossroad prayers' they may have prayed, but we do know their choices.

Abel became a keeper of sheep, and Cain a farmer, a worker of the ground. How important, how essential their labours in those early days of our human race. How important today in our world, still contending with famines, poverty and basic life needs.

Beyond the labour, these brothers also learned that their work was first of all to serve God, --a higher dimension of their labours. So they brought him an offering: "Cain brought to the Lord an offering of the fruit of the ground, and Abel brought of the firstborn of his flock." (4:3f)

Can we see it, can we say it, that what is best, and wonderful about their work as farmer and shepherd was in the way it belongs with worship, thanksgiving, and praise to God?

Wherever your crossroad prayers take you, whatever work, career, trade or profession, the best and brightest experience will be offering your work-life to God in thanksgiving and praise, and in some way giving to him the first and best of all he gives you.

Whatever our labours, and however high- or low-regarded, they become something greater and better as part of our worship. The Psalmist saw it: "What is man that you are mindful of him, and the son of man that you care for him? Yet you have made him a little lower than the heavenly beings and crowned him with glory and honor. You have given him dominion over the works of your hands... O Lord, our Lord, how majestic is your name in all the earth." (Psalm 8:7-9)

Thank you, Lord, that anything I do can be much bigger and better than I can imagine. Please show me what this means for your work-world call upon my life. Amen

Crossroad Prayers

DAY 19. BROTHERS, SISTERS, KEEPERS

Genesis 4:8-16

Seeking and finding our life-work we naturally think first of our own benefits. Learning to understand our work as serving and worshiping God raises it all to a higher level, that other dimension. Again, God wants our work to be something far better and greater than hard labour stuck in 'eating your bread by the sweat of your face.' God's ways are better than our ways.

This means a steep learning curve for us all, as it was for Cain, who had a problem in his relationship with God and with his brother. Something was not right in his heart and so his offering was not accepted by God. Abel's offering, and heart was right, and was accepted. More than this we do not know. But "Cain spoke to Abel his brother. And when they were in the field Cain rose up against his brother...and killed him." (Gen. 4:8)

Murder in the workplace, and in the heart, not necessarily about the work. Pressures, stresses, personality conflicts, on the job; it happens often in our world, too, even a sudden urge to "kill somebody." Killing happens, too, sometimes with a look, or a weaponized word.

Once more our crossroad prayers for where God would have us go in the work world need to include thoughts of what the day to day life together could be like in our workplace. And we need to pray not with fear or apprehension, but with knowledge of how good it can be to learn, with God, to work together in good relationships.

Just one small person in a large company, I am quite limited in what I can do; but if God is in it, I can have great expectations. Cain and Abel did not learn this as brothers or as workers, but if we pay attention to them, and hear God's voice, we can.

God asked Cain, "Where is Abel your brother? Cain answered, "I do not know; am I my brother's keeper?'" (4:9) His heart probably knew the answer to the question, though we don't hear it. There are unique and

Crossroad Prayers

important ways in your workplace where you can know how you can be your sister's, your brother's "keeper," helper, friend, encourager, and it will always in some way work for the good of everyone around-- even for business.

Lord, as I pray about my workplace maybe I need to pray about the people I work with and what this means for my decisions. Amen

DAY 20. ADAM'S TV

Genesis 4:17-26

I wonder if Cain's children or their children's children asked God about their life work. His son Enoch "built a city;" that must have been quite a life-project. One called Jabal, Cain's great-great-great grandson "was the father of those who dwell in tents and have livestock." His brother Jubal was into music, "the father of those who play the lyre and pipe." Then we read of Jubal's half-brother Tubal-Cain, whose work was forging "instruments of bronze and iron."

Was God included in these life work choices of our ancient ancestors? We cannot say, but it doesn't look like their father and grandfather Cain gave them much help.

Genesis 4 turns us back again to Adam and Eve and another son, Seth. And Seth had a son, Enosh. We aren't told of his chosen work, but we are told, "At that time, people began to call upon the Name of the Lord." (4:26) This line of the family found for their lives the way of prayer, 'calling on the Lord,' and so walking with God. In this tiny glimpse into their lives God again calls us to call on him, and to walk with him in our daily living and at our crossroads.

If the name of the Lord had been in Enoch's heart, the city he built would have been a community of blessing. So also with Jabal's life as nomad and herder, and Jubal's world of music making, and Tubal-Cain's metalworks. "A faithful man will abound with blessings." (Proverbs 28;20)

These very short stories of our early ancestors are intriguing, but have the feel more of the "sweat of the face" struggle, than of the bright promise of God's call to dominion in his name over the earth.

I can't forget what one of my professors many years ago said about Adam and God's 'dominion call.' Those were the days when the TV industry was still new, and TV sets were showing up in every living room. My prof was reflecting on how Adam's broken relationship with God somehow broke everything in us, not least of all our clear thinking, our gaining knowledge, and our scientific dominion in our world. If it were not for sin, he said, Adam would surely have figured out how to do television.

Expand my thinking, Lord, of what your first call to 'have dominion' can mean for my own calling. Thank you, Lord

DAY 21. WHEN YOUR NAME IS CALLED
Matthew 1:18-21

You are in the waiting room or outer office, thinking about your application for an interview for a job, or a course of study. Your name is called, so you stand up and walk toward the interviewer's office or desk. What will come of this call-out of your name? Maybe little, or maybe a new world awaits. Maybe it will be another learning experience, or maybe, in and through this conversation will come the next step of Jesus' call for your life, your future.

Once somehow beyond time and space Jesus' name was called. He was called out of the heavenly kingdom and sent --right here, to us and our bloody planet. Jesus very name held, contained his calling. In a dream an angel told Joseph of the child Mary 'had conceived in her from the Holy Spirit.' "And you shall call his name Jesus, *for he will save his people from their sins.*" (Matt. 1:21)

In Greek his name is Jesus; in Hebrew Joshua, or "Jahweh is salvation." Jesus' name held within it our whole world, its people, and his salvation work here among us.

"For God so loved the world that he gave his only Son. that whoever believes in him should not perish but have eternal life." (John 3:16) "He came to his own, and his own people did not receive him. But to all who did receive him, who believed in his name, he gave the right to become children of God." (John 1:12f)

Jesus' call and your call may seem hard to connect, even "a bridge too far,"--but not so! His call for you is a call into his own salvation work, gathering people to God, also in your workplace. We cannot see how all the pieces fit together, but he sees and knows it very well. And calls you.

Lord, it is too much for me to grasp, how my work life can be part of your work of salvation- life; but please help me simply trust you, and follow, one step at a time. Thank you

DAY 22. IMMANUEL AND YOUR WORKPLACE
Matthew 1:22-25

Jesus had another name, given in Isaiah's writing: "Behold, the virgin shall conceive and bear a son, and they shall call his name *Immanuel* (which means, **God with us**). Matt.1:23

God knew very well that no one on earth, no matter how diligently they searched, would ever, ever find him. So God, 'who loved the world so much' in Jesus came very close, right into our world, into our humanity, and wherever allowed, into our lives. He came into Adam's world of death, and he brought life, the 'second Adam.'

By his name *Immanuel* we learn to know Jesus better, and the work he came to do. At the same time we learn more of the work we are given and sent to do. In your crossroad prayers he reminds you that he is sending you into your world, and your workplace world, to be his own woman, his own man, precisely there. As Jesus is in you, so will he be God with the people around you--Immanuel again.

So as you pray crossroad prayers, for the best pathway of work, career, or study, know that *Jesus Immanuel* means being fully *with and for* the people you are serving--in your work of research or design, of producing or retailing, and of knowing clients or customers' needs, and 'making it happen' for them.

God himself is doing this all the time, for everyone, everywhere: he "gives to all mankind life and breath and everything." (Acts.17:25) And he gives without asking first if they love him.

So it is with Immanuel people, and so it is with you in your calling, to serve like God serves, and showing your clients or customers what God is like, even when you cannot speak his Name. He is still always Immanuel with you and with the people of your workplace.

Crossroad Prayers

Lord, I don't know if this "God with us" word narrows my search, or if it makes any road I am considering more or less likely or appealing. But I need to know how to be Your presence there. Thank you, Jesus Immanuel.

DAY 23. PERFECT WORD

Matthew 4:1-4

Jesus, the second Adam, before he began his work, was led, not into a garden but into the wilderness "to be tempted by the devil." (Matt. 4:1) We can never really escape that disastrous beginning of our human race in Eden, and our history, but we can be set free from it.

Also, if we are to discover our own calling as followers of Jesus we must look closely and learn all we can from his own calling. And we see that Jesus' calling, his work, could not begin without a confrontation with the enemy, that 'serpent whose head was to be crushed,' or without Jesus' own time of trial, the fight over his calling, his mission.

For Eve and Adam it was about the fruit. For Jesus it was bread,--which he had not eaten for forty days. It seems that the stomach, hunger, taste are often the focus of temptation!

For Jesus, as for our first parents, temptation begins with a question. The words "If you are the Son of God…" question Jesus' relationship with his Father. Could he be led to doubt it? Is that really who you are? So if you are the Son of God, "Command these stones to become loaves of bread." (v/3)

Unlike our parents in the garden, Jesus quickly caught the lie, refused a conversation, and spoke the truth, simply quoting his bible: "It is written, 'Man shall not live by bread alone, but by every word that comes from the mouth of God." (v.4)

We too must learn to catch the lie, and also to speak the truth--to the devil, also to ourselves, and to one another, and to live only by 'every word from the mouth of God.'

Our crossroad prayers will always be in part about this kind of temptation--if not turning stones into bread, then about how much bread, how much the pay, how high the lifestyle.

Crossroad Prayers

Reasonable pay for our labor is God's will and belongs in our prayers, but not the devil's lifestyles or lies.

If we are followers of Jesus we are learning to build everything upon his word, his written word, which he speaks into our struggles, into our temptations, and into our crossroad choices. This word brought Jesus through to peace and into his work, and this word will bring you through also, all the way.

LORD, speak your right word for today and for tomorrow. In my heart I know that you have it and will give it. Help my listening and my hearing. Amen

DAY 24. GOD'S HONOR
Matthew 4:1-7

As we pray from our crossroads for Jesus to show us the way to our workplace, we will probably never be completely free of the bright and beautiful temptations to fame and glory, or at least a desire to be recognized, honored and praised. Jesus in his wilderness confrontation with the devil had to deal with it.

First came the same questioning of his relationship with his Father, "If you are the Son of God…" and then some kind of vision in which Jesus was taken to the holy city, where he was placed on the pinnacle of the temple, and heard the devil say, "Throw yourself down!" (It has been noted that the southeast corner of the temple was some 300 feet above the floor of the Kidron Valley.) What breathtaking drama, what spectacular fame! Then the devil's clincher: "Throw yourself down, *for it is written,* 'He will command the angels concerning you… and on their hands they will bear you up, lest you strike your foot against a stone.'" (vv. 5, 6) The devil knows the Bible too, and how to twist it into a lie.

Jesus again speaks scripture in its plain truth, and shuts the temptation down. Jesus told him, it is also written, 'You shall not put the Lord your God to the test." (v7)

Jesus' words are important for our crossroad prayers, because we can twist words too, and pray for something we long for, hoping that the Lord might come around to it. Or we can turn and follow Jesus, imitate him, because we have the very same written word he had, the same fighting words, and the same authority.

More than that, from the same Psalm the devil used we are given God's own word about protecting and honoring his people, and hearing prayers: "Because he holds fast to me in love, I will deliver him; I will protect him, because he knows my name.

Crossroad Prayers

When he calls to me, I will answer him; I will be with him in trouble; I will rescue him and honor him. With long life I will satisfy him and show him my salvation." (Psalm 91:14-16) What greater honor could we imagine?

Lord, you understand me when I desire great things, and to be praised. Help me see better the emptiness of the world's honors and praise, and the life-filling joy of yours. Amen

DAY 25. GOD'S GLORY, NOT THE WORLD'S
Matthew 4:1-11

As the Olympics come around every four years, winter and summer, many enjoy watching the events and the athletes, and counting the medals. But the enjoyment, for athletes, fans, and spectators seems so often to turn into a will to dominate the events, the sports, and "own the podium." And some adulation?

The devil told Eve that she could be like God, and so he tells us all. We have it in us, the desire to be some kind of a god. And so with Jesus, when "The devil took him to a very high mountain and showed him all the kingdoms of the world and their glory. And he said to him, 'All these I will give you if you will fall down and worship me." (v.8, 9)

Luke adds, (about the kingdoms and the glory), "it has been delivered to me, and I give it to whom I will." (Luke 4:6) "Prince of this world," he is called, and it is a half-truth.

This temptation, which captured Satan, seems hard-wired in us and shows up in every field of life and of work, in any business, any profession, any human venture--to be some kind of god.
Again, Jesus in this moment saw through it, and said, "Be gone, Satan! For it is written, 'You shall worship the Lord your God and him only shall you serve." (v.10)

The often-quoted words of missionary and Olympian Eric Liddell almost sing his joy in God and his gifts, and his running as worship: "He made me fast, and when I run, I feel His pleasure!"

However the temptation may show up in your mind, you are ready for it with Jesus' words. How good and freeing they are! Does he call some followers into the sports industry?

Crossroad Prayers

Lord, sometimes I don't feel like I'm worth much; other times I want to look down on everybody. Help me see the truth, and help me see how great it is to be your servant. Amen

DAY 26. LIBERATION CALL

Luke 4:16-21

Jesus' wilderness time, and can we say, his crossroad prayers (?) clearly renewed him in his call, his mission, and "He returned in the power of the Spirit to Galilee..." (Lk.4:14) "From that time Jesus began to preach, saying, 'Repent, for the kingdom of heaven is at hand." (Matt. 4:17)

Your crossroad prayer times may sometimes feel like a wilderness, where you cannot see even a dusty trail. But stay close to him, and the power of the Spirit, and he will give you His good news for your own life and work. See your call in his call. Jesus "Came to Nazareth, where he had been brought up, and as was his custom, he went to the synagogue on the Sabbath day, and he stood up to read, on that day, from Isaiah: "The Spirit of the Lord is upon me, because he has anointed me to proclaim good news to the poor. He has sent me to proclaim liberty to the captives and recovery of sight to the blind, to set at liberty those who are oppressed, to proclaim the year of the Lord's favor." (Vv. 18f)

Back from his wilderness confrontation with the devil, Jesus takes to the road, takes up his call--and promptly starts to dismember the devil's kingdom. That kingdom is nothing but a prison, and Jesus gives notice that he has come to set free those who are captives and oppressed. His good news for the poor and sight for the blind are liberation too.

Are you ready for your call to his liberating work and mission? He has called some followers, and keeps calling, to many forms of social work, and to legal and justice systems work, like the International Justice Mission, focused particularly on freeing young girls from the slavery of brothels, in many parts of the world. He has called some to liberation work in addiction-prisons like drugs or pornography. At the same time he always calls his followers to live with the good news of repentance and forgiveness of sins, which is the heart and center, and the beginning of all human liberation. This good word is not restricted to public preaching, important as that is; the Gospel belongs everywhere, in our lives, and in Jesus' way and times--in our workplaces.

Crossroad Prayers

Lord Jesus, it sometimes seems too much to connect my vocation with your world mission, your liberation work. You have to show me what it all means, and what it means for me, personally. Thank you, Lord

DAY 27. HAPPY CONFESSION

Matthew 16:13-20

Jesus calls his disciples and sends them--sends us--into the world's workplaces: the businesses, the universities, the trades, the laboratories, the government offices, to be his servants there. Remember this in your crossroad prayers.

It was into a thoroughly pagan city, Caesarea Philippi, and far from their Galilee ministry, that Jesus had taken his disciples, and faced them with his hard and most important 'exam question:' "Who do you say that I am?" Do you really know me, he was asking. They told him what the people were saying, but these disciples were the ones who had to know him, know who he really was. Simon Peter, quick to speak up, blurted it, "You are the Christ, the Son of the living God."

Jesus gave a ringing 'yes' to the confession: "Blessed/happy are you, Simon bar Jonah! For flesh and blood has not revealed this to you, but my Father who is in heaven!" (v.17)

And this is the foundation stone for everything Jesus would do: "On this rock I will build my church, and the gates of hell shall not prevail against it." (v.18) Here is where Jesus' liberation of people from Satan's prisons begins--with Jesus, God's anointed Christ, and with every follower/confessor of the Name, wherever they go, wherever we go. That's the plan.

Here is part of Jesus' answer to your crossroad prayers: wherever he sends you, whatever workplace-- you belong to him, your Lord; you stand with him, you walk with him. This is your confession. It's not about making noise and calling attention to yourself, or being a super-holy nuisance. It is about the quiet power of his presence in your presence, and your walk in whatever workplace he shows you.

Crossroad Prayers

Help me learn, Lord, that there are times to speak your name, but that this only any good when my life belongs to you and confesses you. Thank you

Crossroad Prayers

DAY 28. UNLOCKING PRISONS
John 20:19-23

Are your crossroad prayers big enough? We all want to learn to pray *bigger* --not pray bigger things for ourselves, but to pray as befits God's great and wonderful plans for the world he loves, and for all whom he calls to follow him. What he is doing through his people is always "more than we can ask or imagine."

Jesus has something more to tell us about his work of liberation for the captive and oppressed people of our world. It may be more than we can ask or imagine, but there it is. He said it first to Peter, but later to all his disciples: "I will give you the keys to the kingdom of heaven, and whatever you bind on earth shall be bound in heaven, and whatever you loose on earth shall be loosed in heaven." (Matt. 16:19) And: "If you forgive the sins of any, they are forgiven; if you withhold forgiveness for any, it is withheld." (John 20:23)

Jesus sends his followers out into their world, with the keys, to set free the captives and the oppressed, free first from their sin and guilt, which is the *inner prison that* creates so many other prisons.

Jesus' call and command is much larger and farther-reaching than Sunday-morning Church, even with all the important, good and vital things that can happen there. The keys of forgiveness and liberation are to be carried 'in our pockets, in our hands, in our minds and hearts as disciples wherever we go in our everyday lives, including our workplaces.

Jesus has much more to teach us about the keys, but he wants us to learn the joy, the mind-bending opportunity, of being part of his work of liberation--and being, with his word, the only real threat to the keeper of the prisons--because we are people standing with heaven's keys in hand-- the forgiveness of sins.

Crossroad Prayers

The more faithful and trustworthy you are in the work, the job, the profession where He places you, the greater the blessing you will be to those around, also for their freedom.

Help me Lord to find my work, and to enjoy doing it well. Help me always remember the work you will do through me, even in setting someone free. Amen

DAY 29. LIKE ROCKY

John 1:35-42

Jesus' work of liberation can be seen wonderfully in his names: *Jesus* means salvation; *Immanuel* means God's very presence in our world. Christ Jesus is the one and only Son of the Father, our Saviour, present with us to save.

Could something like this be true for you? Could your calling, your work be seen also in your name? Maybe it is hard to believe that God has a clear purpose and plan, a task, a work for you to carry out in and by your life, a work nobody else could do, as with Jesus' first disciples, like Simon.

There were two that day who heard John the Baptist say, "Behold, the Lamb of God!" and they followed Jesus as he invited them to the place he was staying. "One of the two who heard John speak and followed Jesus was Andrew, Simon Peter's brother. He first found his own brother and said to him, 'We have found the Messiah (Christ).' He brought him to Jesus. Jesus looked at him and said, 'You are Simon the son of John. You shall be called Cephas (which means Peter)'"

Cephas is Aramaic, *Petros is* Greek, and both mean *rock.* Simon Peter doesn't look like rock in these early days, but he follows Jesus and grows into his name: Cephas, Peter, "Rocky" We see it in the book of Acts, and in his letters. How did you get your name? Some people name children from the Bible, or from God's promises, probably most are named for family or other reasons. But your name does have meaning you don't know about, but which may hold something of God's plan for you.

I have a book, *15000 Great Baby Names.* One of the first girls' names is *Abigail*, a Hebrew name, which means "my father rejoices." For whatever reason a parent may name a daughter Abigail, God also has his own plan, which fits the child, the woman perfectly with a calling to bring joy to her heavenly Father and to her parents also.

Crossroad Prayers

The first name in the boy's section is *Aaron*, "from Hebrew, *Aharon*" and it weans "teaching, or singing" What kind of life of teaching or singing might a boy named Aaron have in God's plan? God knows and he will show it.

In your crossroad prayers would you like to ask the Lord Jesus about your own name, what it means for knowing who you are, and who you will become?

Thank you Lord for my parents who named me; but help me also hear you speak my name. Help me hear from you who I am and who you want me to be. Amen

DAY 30. HE KNOWS YOU

John 1:43-51

Are your crossroad prayers sometimes heavy and hard, or do they sometimes light up with a kind of excitement? Excitement and energy will come from learning Jesus' name for you and his purpose for your life, a purpose and a place that no one else could fill. Because he loves you, he knows you, and knows where you belong.

During one of Jesus' earliest ministry days he found Philip, and Philip found Nathanael, and told him about Jesus. Nathanael was not impressed. But Jesus saw him and said, "Behold, an Israelite indeed, in whom is no deceit!" (Jn 1:47) Nathanael said to him, 'How do you know me?' Jesus answered him, 'Before Philip called you, when you were under the fig tree, I saw you.' Nathanael answered him, 'Rabbi, you are the Son of God! You are the king of Israel!'"

Jesus saw Nathanael, he saw him and he knew him, that he was a man open and honest, who would speak his mind, one no doubt whose 'yes' was yes, and whose 'no' was no. Jesus knows all his followers, every single one whom he has called, or ever will. He doesn't here give Nathanael a new name (the Gospels give him another name, (Bartholomew). But Jesus can read him and knows him well, and his place among the twelve.

He also knows you, and this is your first reason to follow him closely in your crossroad prayers. Friends and family may know you, and may be helpful in working through your work-life decisions, but only Jesus knows you completely, and he is the one who tells you something like he told Nathanael: "Because I said to you, 'I saw you under the fig tree' do you believe? You will see greater things than these!"

David long ago learned this: "O Lord, you have searched me and known me!"   You know when I sit down and when I rise up; you discover my thoughts from afar… You... are acquainted with all my ways. Even

Crossroad Prayers

before a word is on my tongue, behold, O Lord, you know it altogether." (Psalm 139:1-4)

David didn't know what the next day would bring, but he prayed, "In your book were written, every one of them, the days that were formed for me, when as yet there was none of them." (v.16)

These are Jesus' words for you in your crossroad prayer time.

Thank you, Lord, it is good to remember that you love me and you know me completely; it is good to watch and to wait and to listen for my next steps on my way. Amen and amen

DAY 31. ENERGIZED BY WORK?

John 4:1-34

I can remember what someone I know once said, who had just started a job as a teacher, enjoying all the preparation study and looking forward to the next days' teaching and learning time, and thinking "I even get paid for it!" Some such thoughts likely come to most people looking for their job, career, profession, and praying for work they can enjoy--and also get paid for!

Jesus' disciples had gone into Sychar-town in Samaria to find some lunch, while Jesus stopped by the ancient well of Jacob for an unlikely conversation with a woman with her water-jars. After their impactful conversation she hurried back to town and told her neighbours about this amazing rabbi: "Can this be the Christ?"

Jesus' disciples brought him something to eat, "But he said to them, 'I have food to eat that you do not know about... my food is to do the will of him who sent me and to accomplish his work." (Vv32-34)

Jesus' work--calling people to life-- was nourishment, energy, and joy because this was what his Father had sent him for. This was life-giving for him also because it was life-giving for those Samaritans, and for everyone.

Jesus wants a nourishing and energizing work for you, too, work that, whatever the field, it will be doing the will of Jesus who sends you, and in some way your own life-enhancing work. A cushy, well-paid and self-serving job or profession will never be enough. The possibilities of the work he gives you are utterly unlimited.. It might be in science, business, medicine, education, agriculture, journalism, art, music, law...and on and on, 'more possibilities than you can ask or imagine.' Your food, your nourishment and your energy is to do the will and accomplish the work of Jesus who sent you.

Crossroad Prayers

Lord Jesus, are my crossroad prayers cramped by my desire for work that is too small, too easy, too comfortable? To see my work-calling like you saw yours--is this too much to ask? Thank you

DAY 32. LOVE SHAKING THE WORLD
Luke 9:51-56

Your name, what does it mean to you, and for your life and vocation? Let's think about this again. Does Jesus who calls you give, in your *name* something of his purpose for you?

Jesus gave the Zebedee brothers a name, or a nickname, He called them "sons of thunder." He saw in them a strong will and a spirit that could sometimes thunder. Like that day on the border of Samaria: "(Jesus) sent messengers ahead of him, who went and entered a village of the Samaritans, to make preparations for him.

But the people did not receive him, because his face was set toward Jerusalem. And when his disciples James and John saw it, they said, 'Lord, do you want us to tell fire to come down from heaven and consume them? But he turned and rebuked them." (Lk 9:52ff)

Jesus saw a stormy personality and spirit in these 'thunder brothers,' but he saw also what He could do with them, in them and through them; He could see God's thunder at work in them.

James's thunder didn't last long: "Herod the king laid violent hands on some who belonged to the church. He killed James the brother of John with the sword...." (Acts 12:2)

John's work, on the other hand, lasted for many years, until the nineties of the first century. John learned and taught much over all those years, most especially about the depths and the heights of the Father's love, so very present in Jesus. It was John who wrote those words "God is love," and revealed to us that God's love, real love, is seen only and fully in Jesus and his cross, his bloody love with his life-giving and life-changing power. Softened thunder.

Crossroad Prayers

Jesus, who calls you by name, has a purpose for you, as he did for James and John, and his world-shaking love is at the center of it. I don't know if this helps you find your vocational pathway, but it will if you stay with it.

We can all confess and pray with David "The Lord will fulfill his purpose for me; your steadfast love, O Lord, endures forever. Do not forsake the work of your hands." (Psalm 138:8) Amen, so be it

Day 33. THE GOOD NEWS--HOWEVER

Acts 18:1-4

There is a special joy in coming home, or meeting friends and bringing an announcement of good news. "I got the job!"--or a position in the company, or a place in the study program or a scholarship. Jesus' call to his followers is to bring the ultimate, the greatest possible, the world's only *good news*,--the Gospel of Christ Jesus, and its joy, to our world. So it was in the beginning, so it is today.

For some the call becomes what is often described as a "full time job" of preaching and teaching the good news. For most the call is to live with the Gospel and to carry it into our lives, our communities, *and* whatever workplace we are given. For some, as with St. Paul, the call is to spread the good news wherever sent and to pay the bills by working at a trade or profession. After preaching/teaching in Athens, Paul "...went to Corinth. And he found a Jew named Aquila...with his wife, Priscilla... and he went to see them, and because he was of the same trade he stayed with them and worked, for they were tentmakers by trade.... (As a rabbi Paul was required to have a trade) And he reasoned in the synagogue every Sabbath, and tried to persuade Jews and Greeks."

Paul wrote about this also to the Thessalonian church: "For you remember, brothers, our labor and toil; we worked night and day, that we might not be a burden to any of you, while we proclaimed to you the Gospel of God." (1Thess.2:9) Which was his 'day job?'

Your crossroad prayers are full of questions, and you try to listen. Has Jesus said to you anything about what is still called "tentmaking ministry," supporting your Gospel ministry by your skills and employment? Are you hearing a call to focus on the preaching or teaching, and simply trusting God to pay the bills?

For some, that is his way. Or are you hearing a call to live out Jesus' good news in a salaried workplace he shows you? Whatever your call, you want to keep the joy of Jesus' good news in the middle of it.

Crossroad Prayers

Lord, I want to thank you for a work life that is filled with the good news; but you have to show me my way. Amen

DAY 34. WORK AND WORSHIP

Romans 12:1-2

In your life as a follower of Jesus, how close, how connected are your Sundays and your Mondays? That is, how close, how connected are your worship and your work? You probably sense how important and also how good a close connection could be. St. Paul shows us such a connect: "For you remember, brothers, our labor and toil, we worked night and day (at his trade) while we proclaimed to you the gospel of God." (1 Thessalonians 2:9)

Maybe this connection was in his mind when he wrote six or seven years later to the house churches in Rome: "I appeal to you therefore, brothers, by the mercies of God, to present your bodies as a living sacrifice, holy and acceptable to God, which is your spiritual worship." (Rom. 12:1)

Paul remembered well the 'old style' Jewish worship, and could see in his mind all those pieces of bovine and other animal flesh on the altar and the fire; but for Christian worship it was to be the believer's *living self*, the whole person offered in worship. This means that everything we do can be true worship, not only what happens in church meetings.

Paul's tentmaking work and his proclaiming the gospel seem very close, and our Lord's Day worship and our Monday morning work can be very close, too. As the joy of Jesus' good news comes to fill our lives, our thinking and serving, it might even become hard to tell the difference between worship and work.

Maybe thinking this way feels a little wild, even weird, maybe also wonderful. A 17th century Carmelite monk, who took the name Brother Lawrence when he joined the community, where he worked in the kitchen. He called himself "the lord of pots and pans." His whole life was learning what the title of his little book said, *"The Practice of The Presence of God"* --for him, most of all in the kitchen, where his work became what he called "the sacrament of the present moment;" as near to Christ with hands in the dishpan as at the Communion table. Brother

Crossroad Prayers

Lawrence learned over many years to make worship and work the same thing.

Work and worship as the same thing is a long, long way from "TGIF" or being stuck in the "Monday morning blues" syndrome. Praying all this in your crossroad prayers may be a walk on the wild side--God's wild, not the world's,--wild and wonderful. Who knows, his call for you too might be to a kitchen somewhere!

Lord, can you help me see my whole life as real worship, offering myself to you as a very live sacrifice--including my workplace, wherever that may be? Thank you

DAY 35. MORE ON THE WILD SIDE

Following Jesus, learning to give your body, your whole self to him as a live sacrifice, and learning to make your work and your worship the same thing, is truly a "walk on the wild side." But to our world everything Jesus does is wild. So Paul says: "Do not be conformed (shaped, molded) to this world." Instead, "Be transformed by the renewal of your mind." (Rom. 12:2)

As Jesus' followers we are in his total rehab project, his own work of transformation, and we want to remember that as we pray our crossroad prayers. As we pray and follow step by step, and do what he says, we "by testing...discern what is the will of God, what is good and acceptable and perfect." *Good* and *acceptable* and *perfect:* isn't this exactly what you want for your life's work (or works)?

Sure, praying this way is too much for us, but that's okay; Jesus smiles and says, "Get used to it!" Learn to pray all his good things; you don't want to miss any. This wild praying and following is life in Jesus' kingdom of heaven, which he also says is "Like a treasure hidden in a field, which a man found and covered up. Then in his joy he goes and sells all that he has and buys that field." (Matt.13:44) It is like that pearl merchant "Who, on finding one pearl of great value, went and sold all that he had, and bought it." (Matt.13:46)

Such selling out is Jesus' wild way, and this is how we "discern what is the will of God, what is good and acceptable and perfect. As we follow him, walk with him, he transforms us and renews our minds. This makes no sense to the world we live in, but that is the world we don't want to fit or look like.

It takes a lot of prayer time to keep your balance, and keep your feet on the right path, but it can be done--anyone following Jesus can do it. You can do it. And so you will discern the good, acceptable and perfect will of God, for your whole life, and for your vocational life.

Crossroad Prayers

Lord, help me see better the great gap between the world's wild and your wild, and how great and good you are, and your ways. Amen

DAY 36. ONE OF A KIND

Romans 12:3-6

What is Jesus' call for me, what is the work, the job, the career, the trade, the profession for me? This is your crossroad prayer, and you pray it, especially because you are unique, one of a kind, or you are discovering this. Some well-known public figure had died, and was being honored, and someone said, "After him, they broke the mold!" -- meaning of course that there would never be another like him. Many do not realize that God doesn't use molds; each person is one of a kind, and even our DNA says it. Best of all, God knows each of us perfectly and has a place and a purpose for each. And so for you.

So, very important for your prayers is what Paul wrote to the Roman church: "For as in one body we have many members, and the members do not all have the same function, so we, though many, are one body in Christ, and individually members one of another." (Vv. 4, 5)

Paul is speaking to us here about the church, all Jesus' called ones, and about every member, called to be his hands and feet, his eyes and ears, used by him with these spiritual gifts to serve and to build his kingdom of faith and life. Paul is not speaking about the world--where we are looking for our vocation--but about the Spirit's gifts.

But *spiritual* gifts are usually closely related to our *natural* gifts and abilities, the things we are good at, and that we enjoy. Discovering, developing and using these natural gifts seems usually where we, where *you*, discover your vocation. Here is where your uniqueness shows up, and also the place, the purpose, the work he has for you. Your place is one nobody else can really fill, yours a work that nobody else can do, at least not in the way, or the place and time he has in mind for you.

Jesus' plan, and his call, makes each person-- makes you-- very important, even irreplaceable, as are a hand, a foot, an eye, an ear. This is true first of all as members of Christ's body, but also as his body at work in the wide world.

Crossroad Prayers

Lord, you know how hard it has been for me to find out who I am; but thank You for your promise to help me, and for what this means for my vocation. Amen

DAY 37. CARDIO CHECK

Romans 12:9-21

Crossroad prayers: as important for knowing ourselves as for finding Jesus' workplace, and as important for recognizing our natural gifts as for living with our spiritual gifts. Paul, again in Romans, tells us what's next with our unique place and work when he writes: "Having gifts that differ according to the grace given to us, let us use them…!" (Rom. 12:6)

He urges us to serve each other as Jesus' people, to "Love one another with brotherly affection…rejoice in hope, be patient in tribulation, be constant in prayer. Contribute to the needs of the saints and seek to show hospitality." (Vv.9-13)

But he also urges us to serve anyone, everyone in our world: "Bless those who persecute you; bless and do not curse them. Rejoice with those who rejoice, weep with those who weep…Do not be haughty, but associate with the lowly…repay no one evil for evil…if your enemy is hungry, feed him; if he is thirsty, give him something to drink." (Vv. 14-21)

Your opportunities to bless those around you, especially those you work for, those you work with, those you serve, are somehow unique, new every day. Such words and acts of love will be a rare, even strange thing in many workplaces, but here again is the wildness of Jesus' work and ways, as he walks with you into your work-world.

The beating heart of your work, as with all his followers, is God's life-giving love. Paul writes the same thing to the Corinthian church about spiritual gifts: "If I speak in the tongues of men and of angels, but have not love, I am a noisy gong or a clanging cymbal." Even if I have all faith "to remove mountains, but have not love, I gain nothing."(1 Corinthians 13:1-3)

Does your heart rate increase sometimes as you pray about your calling? Ask God to keep the heartbeat of his love strong all the way, until you

Crossroad Prayers

hear and know where he wants you to be and to serve, with your own unique mix of gifts, and you own unique way of loving.

Lord, it is so easy think first of myself in everything, also in my prayers; help me stop and think about all the people in my world, and how I can love them by my work. Amen

DAY 38. A PROPHET?

Acts 2:17-18; 1 Thessalonians 5:20

In your crossroad prayers, what have you discovered, learned or confirmed about your gifts? What vocational options are appealing to you, possibly as Jesus' call? St. Paul, apostle and tentmaker names seven spiritual gifts in his letter to the church in Rome: "Having gifts that differ according to the grace given to us, let us use them: if prophecy, in proportion to our faith; if service; in our serving; the one who teaches, in his teaching…" (Romans 12:6f)

Spiritual gifts they are, and given to serve our world, used by God's Spirit to bring people to life, that is, to a relationship with God, the life giver. As we consider the spiritual gifts Jesus wants for us, we naturally think about our natural gifts, and what these gifts tell us about our vocational pathway.

Prophecy is first named. What is prophecy really, and could it be your calling? Early in 2018, after seventeen high school students were killed by a young man with an assault weapon (and after seventeen other school shootings in 3 months), some voices were heard-- young men and women, classmates-- and their faces seen, on TV, on social media, everywhere. These teens had a message, strong, clear and compelling, and a movement began, with a "March for our Lives," held in many cities over the USA and in other countries, hundreds of thousands, calling for an end to the violence, to the flood of weapons, and for safe and secure schools.

These young voices and their strong message started a movement. Time will tell its long term impact, but in all this we may see a *prophetic* word, and perhaps some young people with a *prophetic* gift. The prophetic gift of Romans 12 is the gift of proclaiming Christ, and eternal life, but our communities, not only our schools, but our family life, our health care, our courts and justice systems, our whole economy and commerce, our whole world waits for people with prophetic words and messages that

Crossroad Prayers

birth movements toward peace, healing, justice--and at the heart of everything, the Gospel of Jesus.

Maybe you are one of them.

Lord, show me what it means when something you said sticks in my mind, and I want to tell somebody. Show me if this is about my vocation. Thank you

Crossroad Prayers

DAY 39. SERVANT

1 Corinthians 12:21-23

"Having gifts that differ according to the grace given us, let us use them...if service, in our serving..." (Romans 12:7) We remember that *servant* is the basic job description for all Jesus' followers, but in praying crossroad prayers we think also of the *service industry*, in retail or distribution, in food services and many trades.

Service workers are often belittled, partly because our society, our world, and sometimes Christians, do not look closely at how important are the services and the servants, and partly because of our pride problems. Service industry workers often degrade themselves too, even those who are very good at what they do; and low pay rates are no help, nor are the stresses in their work.

In hospitals everyone recognizes the work of doctors, nurses, technologists, but when an epidemic, a superbug or virus strikes--and they do--suddenly everyone knows how important the cleaning, sanitation and housekeeping workers are.

Jesus' followers, with natural and spiritual gifts of service, will see beyond the stresses and even the pay; they will see the people to serve, people with names, with faces, with a story, people loved by God, whom they can bless with good services and products needed to live well. Jesus' service industry workers will cover their work and those they serve with prayer, and God will do good things. God also hears prayers about inadequate pay.

If your gift is serving, then serve, in that part of the industry that fits you best, with your mix of interests and skills. Jesus has a place for you, a place you will fill better than anyone, and the people you serve will see it too, and if they can see clearly, they will thank God for you.

Lord Jesus, whenever I see you it seems you are serving me. Can I see your joy in it? Show me what I need to learn. Thank you

DAY 40. TEACHER!
Isaiah 50:4-7

"The one who teaches, in (his/her) teaching." (Romans 12:7) Can you remember from your high school years, or from other schools, classes you looked forward to because you enjoyed them, maybe because the subject was fascinating, maybe because your teacher was leading you on an exciting path of discovery, maybe because of how important and valuable was that art or that science or that history you were learning? All this happened because of that *natural* gift of teaching.

The Holy Spirit also gives *spiritual* gifts of teaching to many of Jesus' disciples, so that they can help people see that he is the truth, and the way and the life. God also sends his teachers into our schools, public and private, into universities, and many special schools you have never thought of, --like schools I heard about not long ago, with courses for prison inmates, or for newly-released convicts, men and women facing a difficult world outside prison walls.

These students are standing at their own critical crossroad-- people who need to learn to see themselves as valuable men and women, who should have a valued place in our world, with good and important work to do. 'Ex-cons' need such schools, which means that they need teachers, especially Jesus' Spirit-gifted teachers. The prophet Isaiah writes about the Servant of God, as a teacher: "The Lord God has given me the tongue of those who are taught that I may know how to sustain with a word him who is weary." (v.4)

Here is God's teacher, with heart and mind filled with the wonder, the beauty, the joy of God and His creation, discovered in all the arts and sciences, and leading to the greater wonder of God's kingdom life. Only God's teaching can sustain those who are weary of a life without meaning. Are any bells ringing here, calling you to a classroom, as a teacher?

Crossroad Prayers

Lord, maybe I have thanked you for a teacher who has helped me find my way; or maybe I have forgotten. What do you want to show me about learning and about teaching? Amen

DAY 41. ENCOURAGERS!

1 Thessalonians 5:11

Lord, is there a job, a career, a profession, a vocation that I am meant for, or that is meant for me? Is this your crossroad prayer? What are your gifts, natural and spiritual, and what are these gifts telling you about your best possible workplace?

Another gift St. Paul writes about: "The one who exhorts, in his exhortation." (Rom.12:8) Exhortation is what happens when someone comes along beside you to help you on your way, to strengthen, to encourage. The Greek word (*parakletos*) is the same word that describes and names the Holy Spirit! The Spirit exhorts us to trust Jesus and to follow him all the way.

We all need exhortation and encouragement in most everything we do, in the endless little jobs and tasks, as well as the heavy and demanding ones, and in our everyday attitudes. So exhorters/encouragers are much needed in every workplace, as well as in the search to find one's way.

A song in Kanye West's "*Graduation*" album sounds like encouragement he tried to give to Chicago schoolkids he visited.
Last week I paid a visit to the Institute
They got the Dropout keepin' kids in school
I guess I cleaned up my act like prison do
If not for pledge at least for the principle
They got the CD they got to see me
Drop gems like i dropped out of PE
They used to feel invisible
Now they now they invincible
(Did your realize that you were a champion)
This is the story of a champion
Runners on their mark and they pop their guns
Stand up stand up here he comes
Tell me what it takes to be number 1

Crossroad Prayers

Do you hear encouragement here; to be a champion, to do great things?

Girls and guys in school and at their crossroads, and finding their way to a vocation need exhorters and encouragers wherever they can be found. But our whole society also needs professional exhorters/encouragers; call them counselors. These are workers who know some psychology, some sociology, (and a lot of Bible!), workers who know themselves and human nature, and who know the exhortation and encouragement of the Holy Spirit. They are the ones who want more than anything to help others on their way, in their living and in their calling.

Are you an encourager?

Lord, you know how discouraged I can be. Thank you for the times when a friend, an encourager showed up. What is your good word for me today? Amen

DAY 42. GIVERS LIFESTYLE

Acts 20:32-35

If I am a follower of Jesus, I pray my crossroad prayers, again not just to find a good job, a satisfying vocation, but to find the work that is meant for me, and that I am meant for. And so I ask the Lord about my gifts, natural and spiritual gifts. The gift next named in Paul's 'list' is the gift of *giving*. "The one who contributes, in generosity." (Romans 12:.8)

God is a giver, **the** Giver. "He makes his sun rise on the evil and the good, and sends rain on the just and on the unjust." (Matt. 5:45) God "gives to all mankind life and breath and everything." (Acts 17:25) But we are all meant to be givers, and sometimes we do give, and it feels good, but we probably feel that we need to learn it better. Or maybe you are one with the *gift* of giving, one Jesus calls to "let it all go," to give freely, wherever, however he shows you.

If you have the gift of giving what kind of vocation or profession might Jesus bring to mind? *The Message* translates this verse: "If you're called to give aid to people in distress, keep your eyes open and be quick to respond." Thinking "people in distress" I can't get away from scenes from the Middle East, or Africa or Asia, of refugees from war, famine, natural disasters, and the desperate need for relief workers with the food, water, medicines, clothing.

Relief work requires many skills, organizational and many others; but what could be better or more important than a gift for giving? Does this make sense? Most relief organizers could not give what is needed from their own pockets, but they would know how to find the resources, and how to find other givers.

This is Jesus' kind of call, which comes from his heart for our world, and maybe a special call for givers.

Lord, I often forget about these suffering ones; help me see them as you see them. Is there anything you want me to do about it? Amen

DAY 43. SERVANT LEADER

Philippians 2:5-11

Of all the faces that look back at us from our media screens, most seem to be the *leaders*--in business, in governments, in entertainment, the CEOs, prime ministers, presidents, the moguls whose names are on or behind everything we buy. In your crossroad prayers have you heard or asked about being a leader, about working toward being head of the company, or the agency, being 'the boss?'

It may be hard to think about leadership when we are still learning Jesus' basic job description of *servant*. But 'Paul's list' of spiritual gifts also addresses "the one who leads," to lead "with zeal." The Greek word means 'to take the position in front' --to lead, to supervise, to manage. Maybe this is another example of Jesus' 'wild ways' --calling some of his followers to become *servant leaders,* as he gives to some of his people leadership gifts, spiritual and natural.

Plainly his church needs servant leaders who follow him who is head of the body. But how badly our whole world, businesses, corporations, city and national governments, our schools, hospitals and every other body, need Jesus' servant leaders. Our world needs his kind of leaders who servant-lead "with zeal," --not zeal for themselves, for power, influence, wealth--but for the corporations/bodies they serve, and all the people the corporations are supposed to serve. (Think "public servants, retail services".)

It takes a servant leader with zeal to lead a company to become a community, truly a body, and to use all its members to provide important, needed, and quality goods and services. This kind of servant leaders can reveal Jesus to anyone and everyone he or she works with and works for.

Lord, somebody said that the world doesn't need those people who seek to be leaders, but gifted servants rather, who are asked, called to lead. Lord, are you saying anything to me? Amen

DAY 44. ARMY OF MERCY

Matthew 25:34-36

As we talk with Jesus about our life-work we naturally have in mind a comfortable workplace and a mostly peaceful kind of work. Jesus does not place his people in some hard and trouble-filled workplace because 'it will be good for us,' but he does call all of us to serve in a trouble- filled and suffering world. He calls all of us to do his Father's work!

The prophets and psalmists told of our God, "Who executes justice for the oppressed, who gives food to the hungry. The Lord sets the prisoners free; the Lord opens the eyes of the blind. The Lord lifts up those who are bowed down; the Lord loves the righteous. The Lord watches over the sojourners; he upholds the widow and the fatherless." (Psalm 146:7-90) And Jesus said of his disciples, of those who inherit the kingdom: "I was hungry and you gave me food. I was thirsty and you gave me drink. I was a stranger and you welcomed me. I was naked and you clothed me. I was sick and you visited me, I was in prison and you came to me." (Matthew 25:34-36)

The last spiritual gift on Paul's list is the gift of *mercy,* the gift of the Father's heart, and Jesus' heart for the broken and hurting: the gift of "the one who does acts of mercy, with cheerfulness." (Romans 12:.8)

William Booth was a man who wanted to preach and teach about Jesus to the poorest and neediest people in the cities of 19th century England. Booth, his irrepressible wife, Catherine his children and his followers went to the streets, to alcoholics, morphine addicts, prostitutes, and their troubled friends; they prayed and fed them, clothed them, served them, helped them find a new life, and meet Jesus. Today the whole world (128 countries at least) knows and relies on Booth's followers' present-day work--their war on behalf of broken and hurting people--the Salvation Army. This army and its soldiers have many gifts, but none more important than the gift of mercy.

Crossroad Prayers

We all want to learn the works of mercy, especially "with the cheerfulness" that surrounds them when God is in them (the Greek word for 'cheerful' almost translates as *hilarity*) Jesus has called many followers into many kinds of vocations of mercy. Does anything here resonate with you?

Lord, it is so easy to keep busy with myself and the people close to me that I forget those who are especially broken and hurting, even some nearby. Send your people into ministries of mercy. Amen

DAY 45. SMALL AND IRREPLACEABLE
1 Corinthians 12:12-31

Do you bring into your crossroad prayers some dreams of accomplishing great things, which will amaze your friends, your world? Big dreams are not a bad thing. But Jesus' call, strange as it may seem at first, is for you to do *your thing!* Your thing is the work you were created for, the work only you can do, the work for which God gave you--and gives you--your gifts. So when he calls you to do 'your thing.' it is not for yourself, rather it is to serve and bless your world in the way only you are able.

This is how it is, because you, as with every other Jesus-follower, are vital members of His body. Servant Paul says it: "God arranged the members of his body, each one of them, as he chose. If all were a single member, where would the body be? As it is, there are many parts, yet one body." And: "If the whole body were an eye, where would be the sense of hearing? If the whole body were an ear, where would be the sense of smell?" (Vv 18-20)

For you, as for every member of his body, your position is small, and yet as essential as your eye or your ear. And you, with your gifts and your call, along with every other member of Jesus' 21st century body, are to do his work among those people who are your 21st century world, especially your whole circle of relationships.

Jesus' body is the church and the church is his body, and we need to have a life together, partly to renew and refuel, but also to pray over our work together. He does not call us to get stuck in a corner somewhere, but to get out into this world, which means into the shops and labs, the boardrooms and agencies where our world does its thing. It is where he sends you to do your thing--which is his, his life-changing and multifaceted works of love. Here are the great things which our world needs, and are very much part of your call.

Crossroad Prayers

Lord, it's hard to get a handle on it, not that I am only one of billions, but that you say I am so important and irreplaceable. Show me what it means. Amen

Crossroad Prayers

DAY 46. NOW YOU DO IT

Matthew 10:5-8

Praying your crossroad prayers as a follower of Jesus it is most important to remember those first followers, his twelve, and even try to put yourself in their place. These disciples sometimes didn't seem to have much of a clue as to where Jesus was taking them, but they followed, walked with him day after day; and they watched him and everything he was doing, and the listened to everything he was saying, as he "Went throughout all Galilee, teaching in their synagogues and proclaiming the Gospel of the kingdom and healing every disease and every affliction among the people." (Mark 4:23f)

Of course the Galilean townspeople were amazed at it all, and so were his disciples. But how much more amazed were they when he said to them, in essence, "Now you do it!" "He called to him his twelve disciples and gave them authority over unclean spirits, to cast them out, and to heal every disease and every affliction." (Matthew 10:5)

He gave them simple, straightforward--and no doubt in their minds utterly impossible--instructions; "proclaiming as you go, saying 'the kingdom of heaven is at hand,' heal the sick, raise the dead, cleanse lepers, cast out demons." (Matthew 10:7, 8)

Jesus didn't send them off to some special school or university or seminary; discipleship was their school--their apprenticeship. There are good times and places for special schools, classroom studies, academics, but Jesus' sending them out with his good news and word of healing was their school; and they tried to do as he said, trusting, watching God work, and bring people to life, learning from their mistakes, and from hours of debriefing with the Teacher. There is no other way to learn Jesus' work.

Again, can you put yourself in their place? Actually, the truth is that you are in that place, because you are a follower. You have seen what Jesus

Crossroad Prayers

has done in your world, your life; and you have heard him call you to do his work in your own world, for and with the people he brings to you.

You will know too that all this is too much, it is way beyond you--and that's good. That's the way it has to be, because knowing this opens you and your world to him, to his work, his power, his love, doing his 'good news and healing' work wherever He sends you. Connecting your job, career, vocation with Jesus' call is at the center of your crossroad prayers.

Lord, your words are too much for me. But I guess you are telling me that *no way* is it too much for you; and that feels good. Amen

DAY 47. JESUS' FAMILY BUSINESS
Matthew 12:46-50

Thinking about Jesus' call to his followers to 'proclaim the good news, and heal,' our first question for him in our crossroad prayers is always: how does this call connect with my job, my working career? Is every follower called to be a preacher or teacher or prayer healer? These are obviously basic and essential to Jesus' work, but how many other ways are there to proclaim the gospel and heal people?

Maybe seeing Jesus' work as a family business would help. "While (Jesus) was still speaking to the people, behold, his mother and his brothers stood outside, asking to speak to him. But he replied to the man who told him, 'Who is my mother, and who are my brothers?' And stretching out his hand toward his disciples he said, 'Here are my mother and my brothers! For whoever does the will of my Father in heaven is my brother and sister and mother..." (Matthew 12: 46-50)

Jesus' disciples are the ones doing the will of his Father, and discipleship is his *family business* of living and proclaiming the good news and bringing healing wherever he sends us. So how many and what professions, trades, vocations belong in Jesus' Family business?

I am thinking of friends and disciples who are living and working in some of our world's most difficult and dangerous places, to help improve agricultural methods, and community water supply, and also to help improve community health for children and families. Other disciple friends are teachers of English and literacy, living under the same dangerous conditions to help people learn these important and much-needed skills.

These friends and workers in Jesus' family business proclaim the good news and bring healing by their lives, their presence; they are his hands and his feet in those hard places. Can we think of any profession, any trade or vocation that can't be a part of the family business, or that he is not using right now?

Crossroad Prayers

Lord, where do I best fit into your family business of good news and healing? Do you want to stretch my imagination here? Thank you

DAY 48. THE HEALER

Acts 9:32-35

"And he called the twelve together and gave them power and authority over all demons and to cure diseases, and he sent them out to proclaim the kingdom of God and to heal... And they departed and went through the villages, preaching the good news and healing everywhere." (Luke 9:1-6)

Does Dr. Luke's account of the ministry of Jesus' twelve make you think about the works of healing? So many of those Galilean villagers needed healing, many kinds of healing. How many of your own family, friends, neighbors need healing? Have their hurts, their suffering-- to say nothing of the whole world's suffering-- made you think about studying medicine?

Jesus didn't study medicine, nor did his disciples, and they knew very well that God is our healer, our one and only healer. Jesus' word and touch worked God's healing for more Galileans and others than we can count, and his disciples were right there with him. Our doctors and medical workers today also know how the body heals itself, and human hands and skills do not, and many recognize the Creator's hand in it. But how thankful we are for the amazing discoveries and technologies used by medical science every day for their life-saving and preserving work, wonderfully facilitating God's healing.

So, God being the healer, prayer is always the first thing we do, and so also healing prayer is the work of every follower of Jesus, wherever our life or vocation takes us. But he also calls many to the works of medicine, doctors and nurses, technologists and researchers. And he gives gifts of healing, spiritual gifts, and natural gifts. These medical workers are themselves God's gifts to our hurting and suffering world-- especially the workers who also pray.

Thank God for our call to healing ministry and prayer. Thank God for every disciple he calls and sends into his wonderful work in hospitals and

clinics, in ERs and ORs, in labs and at bedsides. "Bless the Lord, O my soul, and forget not all his benefits,
Who forgives all your iniquity, who heals all your diseases." (Psalm 103:2, 3)

Lord Jesus, when I am well I may forget about those who are hurting; but help me see better your will for our wholeness, and my share, my place in your healing work. Amen

Crossroad Prayers

DAY 49. RAISE THE DEAD

Matthew 9:18-26

With all the guidance counseling you might receive in your search for a life work or career, counseling good or not, one job description you won't hear about is "raising the dead!" But this task is one straightforward part of Jesus' instructions to his first disciples. "These twelve Jesus sent out, instructing them...'Go to the lost sheep of the house of Israel. And proclaim as you go, saying, 'the kingdom of heaven is at hand.' Heal the sick, *raise the dead*..." (Matthew 10:5-8)

'Over the top' it is, for anyone, even for disciples of many years. But Jesus doesn't say anything more about it, or explain it. His words just stand, unchanged, for his followers, his apprentices. I can see only three occasions when Jesus himself raised someone from death (Jairus' daughter, the widow's son from Nain, and Lazarus). Then we remember Peter (raising Tabitha) and Paul (raising Eutychus). There are other accounts over the history of the church, and I expect He will raise someone again, so today's disciples need to watch him, listen, and do as he says.

But most of the time Jesus call seems to be for another kind of raising the dead--a much more difficult kind, because it is calling people's spirits to life, to the life of faith, to the joy of the good news, and to the forgiveness of sins, which is where His life in us begins.

Does this kind of raising the dead open any doors or spark ideas for your life work or career? How many people do you know who in personal struggles, confusion, hurts, or in troubled and hurting relationships, need and want a new life? How many career workers are there around who are ready and available to help, people who care, who can listen, who know some psychology, who know themselves and know something of how God has made us, and how He helps and heals mind and spirit?

Jesus calls and sends many disciples into public and private agencies of healing, into HR and other business positions, into marriage and family counseling, addiction counseling and suicide prevention programs. All these are very real and present ways and means of "raising the dead" to new life, -- and how our world and society need such disciples!

Lord help me see and hear the hurts of those around me, without getting dragged down myself; bring me close to yourself, and your everyday work of raising people to life, and show me my workplace. Amen

DAY 50. INTO COMMUNITY

Matthew 25:35, Luke 5:12-15

Great possibilities, great opportunities--that's what most career hunters are looking for, to earn a good living, or maybe get rich, and to be recognized. Jesus' opportunities are about bringing a better life, a good life to others, and about his kind of riches. We see another kind of new life opportunity when he called his first disciples to proclaim the good news, heal the sick, and *"cleanse lepers."*

Cleansing lepers was about healing, but also about bringing these people who because of their illness had been shut out of their community. "The leprous person...shall wear torn clothes and let the hair of his head hang loose, and he shall cover his upper lip and cry out, 'unclean, unclean,... He shall live alone, his dwelling shall be outside the camp." (Leviticus 13:45f)

A leper approached Jesus, saying, "Lord, if you will you can make me clean." Jesus came right into his isolation and actually touched him, and sent him to the priest to receive his declaration of health, and so freed him to return to life in family and community.

Jesus' call to all his disciples is to bring all sorts of isolated people into His community, his family and also into each one's home community. Have your crossroad prayers brought these kinds of people and needs--these kinds of opportunities--into your mind? People like the homeless man in a west coast city, who came in from the cold and lay his head on a table in a fast-food restaurant for several hours before a food server came over and realized he was dead.

Jesus calls some of his disciples to work in many kinds of community groups, agencies programs, government positions, and faith ministries. His disciples see lepers, strangers, homeless and stigmatized as his kind of opportunities, difficult but full of possibility of hope and praise and thanksgiving.

Crossroad Prayers

Lord, do I sometimes look past the homeless, the outsiders or others so I can get on with my own thing? Can I see these people as opportunities for a good and hopeful kind of work? Thank you

DAY 51. DEMONS DOWN

Ephesians 6:10-20

"Heal the sick, raise the dead, cleanse lepers. *Cast out demons.*" (Matthew 10:8)

Another job description we won't be given by any career guidance counselor, but which Jesus plainly gave to his followers: "Cast out demons!" To understand or explain what this means is about as difficult as "Raise the dead.", but Jesus' disciples should know the demons when we meet them, and also know that casting out demons is not about understanding or explaining, but of fighting, and fighting not with loud and bloody battles, like Hollywood productions, but with the quiet power of Jesus' word.

I remember a *Time* magazine cover from the 1990s telling the story of the Rwanda massacres, individuals and families, hundreds of thousands dead in their homes and in the streets. The writer couldn't explain the evil except to say "the demons are all in Rwanda!" So read the cover.

The apostle Paul wrote to the Ephesian church about the hard struggles of life with the vital reminder: "We do not wrestle against flesh and blood, but against the rulers, against the authorities, against the cosmic powers over this present darkness, the spiritual forces of evil in the heavenly places." (Ephesians 6:12)

Sometimes we contend with personal demons, sometimes with the world's controlling systems by which societies, governments, businesses, institutions function, and sometimes with the lies Satan plants in our heads, which chain us. Plenty of demons all around, but **no fear**--none can stand up against the quiet and perfect power of the word and the name of Jesus.

But what does all this mean for a disciple's crossroad prayers, for your life-work in world which is under the rulers of "this present darkness?" I remember a story of a foreign Minister or Secretary of State, who climbed in to his limo, and his driver asked, "Where are we going?" The official said, "Anywhere; we've got trouble all over."

That's about how it is for Jesus' disciples trying to find their workplace; the enemy can show up anywhere, and our work will always involve the enemy. Which also means that Jesus is always sending his men and women into any society, institution, business, or government to work, to serve--and especially to see through the lies of the enemy, and to frustrate his' work, breaking down the powers of death and bringing in Jesus' works of life.

Lord, help me see past the people who seem to be enemies, and to see the real enemy behind all the troubles and evils, and to see the power of your word. Amen

Crossroad Prayers

DAY 52. JESUS' CROSSROAD PRAYERS

Mark 1:35-36

Even as you pray your crossroad prayers over what your next decision should be, you are following Jesus more closely than you realize. Luke tells us about Jesus' own crossroad prayers, intense prayers about whom he should call to be his closest little flock of disciples, his *twelve*: "In those days (Jesus) went out to the mountain to pray, and all night he continued in prayer to God. And when day came, he called his disciples and chose from them twelve, whom he named apostles." (Luke 6:12f)

We can hardly imagine how important and difficult was this crossroad that he faced, and how urgent his prayer. Jesus' gospel and mission would be carried to the whole world by those apostles--or not. Which of these men should he choose? He could not do anything without his everyday prayers or without this all-night prayer time with his Father.

So he prayed, and then he chose the ones he wanted. He taught them, he trained them, and they did what he sent them to do--and here we are in the 21st century, also, with his help, following him. And here you are, following and praying like Jesus in your own crossroad prayers--with or without the all-nighters.

Discipleship, after all is said and done is simply watching Jesus, hearing him, and doing what he did, and more than anything, praying like he prayed. He even wants to be right there with you in your prayer times, and he is with you, by the Holy Spirit, who 'helps us pray as we ought.' (Romans 8:26)

Lord, thank you for coming so close to help me make decisions; and thank you for helping me learn how to pray. Amen

DAY 53. FATHER

Luke 11:1-13

Say it again, discipleship is simply following Jesus as closely as we can, day by day--and especially in our crossroad prayers, praying as he did. Our prayers are our most important learning time--learning to know him better, and learning how to communicate better. We keep learning how to ask, how to listen, how to confess, how to question, how to unload our troubles.

Jesus' disciples learned this, so we read: "Now Jesus was praying in a certain place, and when he finished, one of his disciples said to him, 'Lord, teach us to pray...'" Just being with him, watching, listening, taking it all in, and above all seeing how close he was to his Father, showed them how much they needed to learn, and how badly they wanted to learn.

Maybe this hunger is what Jesus waits for, and why he was so ready to answer his disciple, without hesitation, without explanations, telling them just "When you pray, say "Father," Jesus prays "Father;" and he teaches us to pray, "Father!"

When we are thinking clearly, and realize what is happening, it takes our breath away! The one and only Son of God is teaching us to pray as children of God! Simply to call, to pray "Father" is sometimes all we can, or need to pray, as in your crossroad prayers when you do not know where to go. "Father!" is sometimes all there is. Our prayers are always much more than the words or requests;; they are about knowing the Father. So one other day Jesus taught them;, "And when you pray do not heap up empty phrases as the Gentiles do, For they think that they will be heard for their many words. Do not be like them, for your Father knows what you need before you ask him. Pray then like this: "Our Father in heaven." (Matthew 6:7-9)

Take Jesus' words here with you in your crossroad prayers.

Crossroad Prayers

Sometimes, Father, I do not know what or how to pray. Help me know from Jesus' words that I am really your child. Amen

DAY 54. HOW GOOD CAN IT GET?

Psalm 19:7-14

What better word, what better help could anyone be given for crossroad prayers than what Jesus said in Matthew 6:6? "But when you pray, go into your room and shut the door and pray to your Father who is in secret. And your Father who sees in secret will reward you."

In your search for a job, a career, a life work, you may have been given helpful ideas or advice by your father or your mother. Maybe you appreciated it, or some of it, or maybe not. God can speak through parents--partly because they know you pretty well. But they do not have the last word. "Our Father," on the other hand, knows you perfectly, and he also knows the very best path for you to take, and that path will be yours--if you are willing to let him have the last word.

Always the biggest question is: do I trust him? Again, our praying is more about knowing God and trusting him than about the answers, and the better we know him, the better we know how good he is, and how good his ways, his pathways are.

Good old David, king and psalmist! He had a hard life, but somehow he kept on learning how good God's ways are, and his joy spills all over Psalm 19. "The law of the Lord is perfect, reviving the soul;" Following God's way brings us to life.

"The testimony of the Lord is sure, making wise the simple;" His path for you is not a guess, it is a sure thing, and wise, not just smart. "The precepts of the Lord are right, rejoicing the heart;" In your work he wants for you this joy--hearing yourself say, "this is just right, it's where I belong." "The commandment of the Lord is pure, enlightening the eye;" Pure means clean and unmixed with the world's values and ways. "...the rules of the Lord are true and righteous altogether. More to be desired are they than gold, even much fine gold, sweeter also than honey…"

Crossroad Prayers

This is your life, when the Lord's way is your way. This is how your eternal Father, who "in secret" hears your crossroad prayers, and wants to "reward you".

Lord, help me see it better--how good you are, and how good your ways. Amen

DAY 55. DISCIPLES' PRAYER

Matthew 6:5-15

Jesus is the one, the only one who can teach us how to pray our crossroad prayers, or any kind of prayer, and the one who teaches us that our praying is about more than getting answers. Praying is our life with him, and with the Father and the Spirit, and this life together is the biggest part of his answers. He wants our job, our profession, our work life to be a life with him. He wants to bring good things, many blessings to your world, through you, through you and your Lord working together.

So Jesus' prayer, the "Our Father" helps us pray seven petitions over your crossroad questions and decisions.

1. "Hallowed be your name." Your employers will always want you to make them and the company look good. Jesus' petition 'jacks this up' to a whole new level, so that God will look good, and in your work God's goodness, truth and beauty will be seen.

2. "Your kingdom come." Here is a prayer that our whole world and your work world come under new management, God's management. He did create us all and everything belongs to him.

3. "Your will be done, on earth as in heaven." This is partly a prayer that you find your right workplace path, but even more that your world may learn how good God is, and how good are his ways ("better than gold, sweeter than honey"), and how important it is for everyone that he has his way with us.

4. "Give us today our daily bread." No explanation needed here--this is what every crossroad prayer is about. Martin Luther said that "daily bread includes everything needed for this life." Food and clothing, and most everything the world's economy is producing and selling. The question remains, what is your part in it?

Crossroad Prayers

5. "Forgive us our sins as we forgive those who sin against us" This petition is for our whole life, and for our work life, and it is always the beginning of everything because God's forgiveness of our sin brings us to life with him; and forgiving each other brings life to our relationships. And some would say that our workplace relationships may be the most important part of the job.

6. "Save us from the time of trial" ("Lead us not into temptation") We are always praying for help here because trials and temptation are never far away, and certainly find us at our crossroads. So Jesus teaches us how to pray our way through and past these hard places and stay close to him.

7. "Deliver us from evil" (or 'the evil one') Jesus reminds us that the enemy is never very far off, and wants to interfere in your crossroad prayers, so he puts this freedom prayer into our thinking, and our hearts and our words.

It is hard to think the way you think, Lord, and easy to forget you. Thank you that your help never quits. Amen

DAY 56. YOUR HOLY NAME

Revelation 4:1-11

"Hallowed be your name," Jesus teaches us to pray. "Holy, holy, holy is the Lord God almighty..."Worthy are you, our Lord and our God, to receive glory and honor and praise...for you created all things, and by your will they existed and were created."

These are not the first words that come to mind as we ask our Lord to show us the way we should go in our career search, but they do belong in first place in everything we do, and they do show us that our life can in some way touch heaven.

Then we have the Psalmist reminding us of our place in all this creation--"a little lower than the heavenly beings," and given dominion over the works of God's hands. He brings us back to our "first call" remembered in Genesis 1--dominion, lordship, management, care, development of the earth--all to show God's glory, honor and praise, his greatness and goodness, to be seen in this planet he put into our hands.

Then we return to the 21st century and stories like the one about the 600,000 square mile mass of plastic trash, called "the Great Pacific Garbage Patch," three times the size of France, and the problem causing the death of more than 100,000 whales, dolphins, turtles, seals, and seabirds every year.

And the story of a young Dutch entrepreneur, Boyan Slat, who created a company called Ocean Cleanup, working with nets and booms to collect the plastic and trash, and help clean our planet. Whatever God's glory, honor and praise mean to this young man, and however successful his efforts may be, he and his company are working for God's kind of dominion over the earth. Here too is another young person with a calling.

Jesus wants your crossroad prayers to be big enough. And they will be if hallowing God's name is in them.

Crossroad Prayers

Open my eyes and my heart to your greatness and your goodness, and help me pray bigger; and help me worship you in my work calling. Amen

DAY 57. GOD RULES!

John 15:7-12

We need Jesus' 'teaching prayer,' our Lord's Prayer, so that we as his disciples can learn how to pray; and every petition he teaches us is important for our crossroad praying. So we pray the second petition: "Your Kingdom come". This means that we want GOD to rule, to rule everything, our whole world, and first of all our own lives, and our work lives.

This is not an easy prayer, because it is plain to see from the evil and suffering, and the violence of our world, that someone else must be ruling, in most places and in most lives. The Bible calls him "the prince of this world." So praying "Your Kingdom come" is plainly an act of rebellion against the devil, and the world that follows him. But this prayer is hard also because it is against ourselves; the ways of this world come so naturally to us all.

But praying "Your kingdom come" becomes a disciples' pure joy too, as we learn how our Lord rules, not by the world's lies and deceptions, manipulation and force, but in love, the mind-bending love of God.

Jesus teaches us how God's rule works: "If you keep my commandments, you will abide in my love, just as I have kept my Father's commandments and abide in his love." (v9f) Then Jesus spells it out, plain and simple: "This is my commandment, that you love one another as I have loved you." So God's kingdom comes. (And he adds: "These things I have spoken to you that my joy may be in you, and that your joy may be full") God's rule covers our whole world, doesn't it, and your personal world, and your work world?

So Jesus searches for disciples who have been given "ruling" gifts-- leadership, management, organization,-- and vision--to be his presence in all kinds of worldly businesses, institutions, and levels of government, and more, and for disciples who are always praying the rebel prayer, "Your kingdom come."

Crossroad Prayers

As our catechisms tell it, God's Kingdom **is coming,** in his way and his time, whatever anybody may think; but as Jesus' disciples we want to be in on it! So we pray today in our crossroad prayers, "Your Kingdom come"-- God rules!

Lord, your rule in this world is too great and amazing for me to understand. Thank you for that; and thank you for calling and bringing me into it. Amen

DAY 58. THE GOOD WILL

John 6:36-40

"Your will be done, on earth as it is in heaven!" Jesus prayed his Father's will, and struggled with it in Gethsemane, when he prayed his "cup," the crucifixion, might not happen; "nevertheless, not as I will, but as you will." (Matthew 26:30) Earlier Jesus said, "I have come down from heaven not to do my own will, but the will of him who sent me." (John 6:28)

So praying this petition of our Lord's Prayer is closely following Jesus. You may have prayed it many times in your crossroad prayers, in your searching, listening to know his word, and the vocation he wills for you. It is another hard prayer, another prayer against one's self, that is, against any self-serving and wrongheaded paths or career possibilities that may tempt. But it is a prayer for his will, not yours, for his work-life plan that fits you, your gifts, and your abilities that he has given, the things you are good at, or know that you could be good at. This prayer is that you may serve the people he wants you to serve.

"Your will be done" is also a prayer for the amazing freedom that comes in your discipleship, as the song has it: "Jesus, all for Jesus… All I am and ever hope to be, all my ambitions, hopes and plans I surrender into your hands. For it is only in your will that I am free." (Robin Mark)

"On earth as it is in heaven". Working God's will brings heaven to earth--and to your part of the earth, to the people in your world of relationships. Human wills and works so often bring hell into many lives, even unintended. But praying God's life-giving will over everything you do, every job, every task, will always bring some touch of heaven into your world.

Thank you that you are working your will in our world; Lord, help me be in on it! Teach me the wisdom of wanting what you want. Thank you

DAY 59. BREAD IS A BIG WORD

Psalm 147:7-15

"Give us today our daily bread," Jesus teaches us to pray. Our crossroad prayers will usually begin right about here, with finding how to put bread on my table. But before I can think about how to do this, Jesus has me praying about putting bread on others' tables. Lord, give **us,** not just me, this bread, day by day. Then, as we pray about the bread for our bodies, perhaps we suspect that we are praying for more than just food. And Luther's catechism spells it out, first with a question: "What is meant by daily bread?" and then with this answer: "Daily bread includes everything needed for this life, such as food and clothing, home and property, work and income, a devoted family, an orderly community, good government, favorable weather, peace and health, a good name, and true friends and neighbors."

Jesus teaches us pray for "everything needed for this life," and not just for me and my household--which is good and important--but for **us,** for all his Father's children, and of course for so many who are not yet his children.

So in your crossroad prayers for the kind of work, career, profession which you trust will provide your basic life needs, you are also asking him to show you the work that will provide for others' basic life needs--a good refresher in our *servant* job description.

The "everything needed for this life" list covers probably every industry, business, trade, or profession you could think of. So this petition may not help you narrow down your options for what work is best for you; but maybe you need a long look at all the options, so that you don't miss out on a possibility that may be perfect for you.

"Give us today..." we pray to God the Giver, who is going to use *your* hands and skills, your labor and your love for *his* giving.

Crossroad Prayers

Again, Lord, help me see my work as part of your work, and help me see how important it is to you, to me, and to how many others? Amen

DAY 60. OUR FOOD AND CLOTHING
Matthew 25:31-40

Praying "Give us our daily bread"--"everything needed for this life," and "food and clothing" as your crossroad prayer might point you straight to a job at McDonald's, or a clothing shop at the mall, and that might be a good place to Start--and maybe stay. But in every prayer we want to remember the "**our**," and that whatever the "food and clothing" work, for Jesus' followers it is focused on the needs of the other people in our world.

How might you serve and bless your neighbors by a career in agriculture or ranching, in food production or marketing, in cooking, baking, serving? Some see special projects like rescuing good food from the waste bins and landfills, and providing healthy food for the many whose money always runs out before the month does. Some want to bless neighbors with clothing, imaginatively designed and manufactured, quality at a fair price, and free of the curse of sweatshop labor.

Some of Jesus' followers can see beyond drudge jobs into endless possibilities of "food and clothing," serving and blessing the world, even as Dr. Seuss' puts it: "O the places you will go!" Imagination, possibilities! Does any of this route out of your crossroad look good, feel right for you?

Jesus helps us know clearly what we are doing when we are serving people in these ways, in his name. He says: "I was hungry and you gave me food, I was thirsty and you gave me drink… I was naked and you clothed me"   "Food and clothing" work can be a joy here and now, as well as at judgement day, when after your years of feeding and covering-- also the times when you were too busy to think of Jesus-- he says, "Truly, I say to you, as you did it to one of the least of these my brothers (and sisters) you did it to me."

As you pray your "crossroad fourth petition"--it's all there.

Crossroad Prayers

Lord, help me see the faces I need to see, of the "hungry, thirsty, naked," and what you want me to do about it. Amen

DAY 61. OUR HOME AND PROPERTY

John 14:1-6

"Give us our daily bread." give us "everything needed for this life," give us "home and property." Here at your crossroad is Jesus calling you to trust him for your dwelling place, and to a life work of helping others to have their dwelling place? As you pray, can you hear him saying anything about housing or construction trades, or design or architecture? What about real estate or finance? Doesn't Jesus send some of his followers into "home and property" industries?

Maybe he shows you the homeless in your town, young and old living on the streets. Maybe he shows you rundown sections of the city being bought up to be turned into high priced condos, and in the process putting more people on the streets. Maybe he shows you refugees in so many places around the world, or next door.

Maybe it is helpful to think about Jesus, the ultimate 'realtor:" "In my Father's house are many rooms. If it were not so would I have told you that I go to prepare a *place* for you?" This "place for you," for his disciples, is beyond our imagination, but he wants us to think about it. At the same time, *place* is important here and now, also: "And she gave birth to her firstborn son and wrapped him in swaddling clothes and laid him in a manger, because there was *no place* for them in the inn." (Luke 2:7) How this family needed a place--for this birth! And God provided it--the stable, the perfect place for Christ Jesus to "come down," all the way down, to live with us!

So Jesus knows how important is your place, your dwelling, and all your neighbors' dwellings, too. So he might send you out as "home and property" worker--one of his own 'here and now' 'realtors' to help some of those neighbors to have the place they need, and that he wants for them.

"Daily bread." "home and property." Any sparks here for your crossroad prayers?

Crossroad Prayers

Lord, you know my ideas and dreams about where and how I would like to live; help me think and dream about the best kind of dwelling for brothers/sisters/neighbors. Amen

DAY 62. OUR WORK AND INCOME
Matthew 6:25-33

We pray for our "daily bread," for "everything needed for this life"-- including "work and income," as the catechism has it. Maybe we can skip this part, since this is what all our crossroad prayers are about? Or do we need to see something more here?

Does Jesus even tell us not to pray about our "work and income," when he says "Do not be anxious about your life, what you will eat or what you will drink, nor about your body, what you will put on?" He says that life is more that. "Look at the birds of the air, they neither sow nor reap, nor gather into barns, and your heavenly Father feeds them." He says, "Do not be anxious" about these life needs. "Your heavenly Father knows you need them all."

So trust him, he goes on, and "seek first the kingdom of God and his righteousness, and all these things will be added to you,"-- all your "work and income" needs. Or maybe Jesus is not asking you to skip the "work and income" prayer, but rather to get rid of the anxiety, and to focus your prayers completely on his kingdom, and your kingdom work. I guess that brings us back to the second petition, "Your kingdom Come," and God's rule here in our world, "as in heaven."

God rules when the Holy Spirit brings us to faith and to following Jesus, and our Kingdom work is to help others do the same. Here, of course is work for "prophets and evangelists, pastors and teachers" (Ephesians 4). But remember that Jesus sends the likes of prophets and teachers not only, not even mainly, to church meetings, but into every place of 'work and income.'

So all our crossroad prayers as disciples are God's kingdom prayers. "For we are God's fellow workers." (Philippians 2:13)

Crossroad Prayers

Lord, can I just give over to you all my jobs and career struggles and anxieties? And what do I need to learn about "seeking first your kingdom" in my work? Amen

DAY 63. DEVOTED FAMILY
Mark 9:1-9

Jesus has us pray for "daily bread"--for "everything needed for this life," and as the catechism has it: "a devoted family." Most people know how important for everyone that home life together as family is; we know it either because we have grown up with a devoted family, or because we have perhaps missed out.

Helping people in our world learn how to have or be 'devoted families' may not come readily to mind in your crossroad prayers as your life work, but it is close to Jesus' heart and to discipleship, and discipleship is a call to life as it was meant to be. So when Pharisees challenged Jesus with a question about divorce, and broken families, Jesus took them--and us--straight back to the beginning, to the family wholeness that was meant to be: "But from the beginning of creation God made them male and female. Therefore a man shall leave his father and mother and hold fast to his wife, and the two shall become one flesh. So they are no longer two but one flesh." (Mark 10:6-8) The two leave home and commit themselves to each other, become one flesh, one in heart and body, and form a new home, welcome children and become "a devoted family," in our world always imperfect, yet one and blessed.

Jesus does call followers who understand and care deeply about family life to a life work or career of working with and for families, for the health and wholeness that come with learning devotion to one another. He calls some to the healing of family life as ministry of the church, and he calls some to public health and social services, family life and counseling, all good and important workplaces to serve the neighbors to whom God sends you.

But he also calls us, many of us, to a life that serves still better and impactfully--in your own marriage, and the devoted family God forms in your home. Anyone who follows Jesus through all the struggles and promises of learning family life will be a light and a joy in the neighborhood, and God's own presence and love in your home will not be missed; it will be seen, and desired; neighbors will want what God has given you. Perhaps 'devoted family' life is an important part of everyone's crossroad prayers.

Lord, we see so much brokenness in families all around, also in our own. Show me your way to the wholeness of devoted families, and how we can help each other. Amen

DAY 64. GOD'S HEART FOR THE BROKEN
John 4:1-30

Praying for a 'devoted family' for yourself, your relatives, your neighbors, and asking if Jesus wants you to work helping and strengthening families as your calling is no easy prayer. It is difficult partly because of the hurt we feel ourselves, and with those closest to us, who are hurting with broken marriages and families; and it is difficult also because so much of our society seems to have lost so much, not only the experience, but even the meaning of "devoted family."

Our 21st-century world stumbles around in much confusion, not only with divorce as the Pharisees challenged Jesus about, but much ignorance and confusion about what "one flesh" means, and what bearing children means, and contradictions like "same-sex marriage."

Jesus' heart, and his Father's heart is always reaching out to us all in our broken and hurting relationships and households. And we are all broken in our own ways. We remember John's Gospel showing this, when Jesus spent a noon hour by Jacob's well with that Samaritan woman troubled with a series of broken relationships. He asked her for a drink of water, and then offered her a better kind of water. He asked about her husband, and then addressed her brokenness: "You have had five husbands, and the one you now have is not your husband." (John 4:18)

The woman tried to change the subject. But Jesus spoke to her heart as she asked about Messiah, and he said to her, "I who speak to you am he." (v.26) The woman was overwhelmed, hurried back to town and spread the word. Much more could be said, but Jesus shows God's heart for broken families. And broken people, and his call to know him and to follow him.

St. John tells also of another day, when "The scribes and the Pharisees brought a woman who had been caught in adultery," and again challenged Jesus: "Now in the law Moses commanded us to stone such women. So what do you say?" …"Jesus said to them, 'Let him who is without sin among you be the first to throw a stone at her.'" Everyone left, and Jesus said, "Woman, where are they? Has no one condemned you? She said, 'No one, Lord.' And Jesus said, 'Neither do I condemn you. Go, and from now on, sin no more.'" (John 8: 7-15)

Here is Jesus' heart for us in our broken marriages, and families, and lifestyles, and his call to meet, to know and to follow him out from the rubble, sin and hurt, and toward his 'devoted family' kind of life. How much of our whole society of broken relationships could be repaired, remade if Jesus had his way?   Nothing is simple, no 'easy fixes,' rather a difficult path, yet truly new life, and very real, because it is his work and he is in it!

What might your life work be, spent on Jesus' 'devoted family' building?

  Lord it seems like there's a war on against devoted families, and it is hard to understand. Help me remember that we are all broken, and sought by you. Show me my path.   Thank you

DAY 65. WHO HEARS THE CRY?

Luke 18:1-8

In our prayer for daily bread the catechism also includes as basic life need "an orderly community" and "good government" and it seems that one requires the other. In teaching his followers to pray Jesus calls us to think about justice, which is at the center of orderly community and good government.

His parable, which maybe you just read, urges his disciples that "they ought always to pray and not lose heart." (v.1) Jesus urges them to pray like the widow he portrays, who kept after her town's judge "who neither feared God not respected man," She would not give up, and kept calling out, "Give me justice against my adversary." Her cry sounds like many Psalms, also calling for God's justice. Jesus' parable is about persistent prayer, but also about the cry everywhere for justice and order, which is also a call for good government.

Does this kind of prayer fit anywhere into your crossroad prayers? Do cries for justice come to mind as you seek your life-work, your vocation? We cringe when we hear reports of lives, families, communities in so many places around the world, destroyed by terrorist groups or dictatorial governments. Also in our democratic societies we hear too often--or experience--injustices from the powers and authorities that run our world. The widow's cry, "give me justice" seems very familiar.

Jesus calls his people to pray, and not give up. But maybe in our 21st century world he also calls some, even you, *to be a judge*! Truly he does call disciples to preside over our courts, and in his name to "give justice to his elect, who cry to him day and night," and for many others whose cries he hears.

Again, he has called more disciples than we know into working for good government, into the courts, all kinds of legal work, and legislation and law enforcement. I can think of a young lawyer, giving most of his time

Crossroad Prayers

to *pro bono* legal aid for the poorest and the powerless, whose cries for justice nobody hears.

Your crossroad prayers might lead you to being yourself an important part of God's answer to somebody's prayer.

Thank you Lord for hearing our hearts' cries for help; and for teaching us to hear. Amen

DAY 66. FAVOURABLE WEATHER!

Genesis 1:26-31

In our prayers for daily bread, and basic life needs the catechism also includes "favorable weather" How often do you pray about the weather? I suppose we all do when important outdoor events, parties, hikes, or celebrations are coming up. In recent years, however, maybe more people are praying--or wondering how to pray--as we live with whole summers of forest fires, or as communities are hit hard with storms, tornadoes, flash floods, streets, homes inundated with water, and records it seems made or broken every year.

Weather and related forms of destruction make me think again of Genesis 1:26, and humanity's 'first call' about 'man in God's image and likeness...and having dominion' over the created world. Arguments are endless over the weather, and over what we humans are doing to affect, or impact the weather. Maybe we are being called to more prayer over the weather-- and our whole environment. How God would love -- overseeing our planet, and us, to say "Well done, good and faithful servant."

But as we stand in our 21st century world, it's not looking good. So we pray over our weather and our planet, for understanding and for wisdom, for ourselves, for our neighbors, and for well-being, all much "needed for this life." Does this prayer somehow belong in your crossroad prayers? We don't need to be told that we are an important part of the answer. We are learning better how we can clean up our planetary house, and change our ways, with small and large things we can do to clean the air, soil and water.

Can you see any connection here with your search for job, career, vocation? It must be hard to find a business or industry that isn't leaving a big, dark footprint on our earth, or a corporation that does not need leaders, managers, laborers who know about the dominion given us over the earth, and our accountability as God's servants.

Crossroad Prayers

We need to thank you Lord for our responsibility to care for our world. Thank you for repentance and forgiveness for failures, and for new beginnings. Amen

DAY 67. DEEP PEACE

Ephesians 4:17-24

We pray for daily bread as Jesus teaches us, and we know this includes all the basic life needs named in the catechism, and maybe more than anything, **peace**, particularly that inner peace of mind and heart, also in your crossroad prayers. Right now you want mind and heart at peace with your pathway to work, career, vocation, the peace of mind that says this is the way, the right way toward the best workplace for you.

But there is a deeper peace that must come first, before vocational, or any other peace. Kanye's *Graduation* album, noted above, included songs which were all about hard life questions and meanings, like finding out who I really am. Here is the deepest peace we long for, whether we realize it or not: knowing ourselves, and more than knowing, being at peace with ourselves, with who we are. It means knowing the good gifts God has given us, knowing how to live in our own skin, and with our own unique personality, at peace.

The Lord wants this for you more than you know, and leads you and every disciple from the difficult crossroad we face every day, where we come to terms with our own self-centeredness--which ruins life--and where he helps us turn around, toward himself and his peace. And "to put off the old self...and to be renewed in the spirit of your minds, and to put on the new self, created after the likeness of God in true righteousness and holiness." (Eph. 4) In this renewal is Jesus' peace.

Here is peace with yourself, the new self you are becoming, and peace in your crossroad prayers, with the life work Jesus shows you, meant to be very much a part of that new self. "My peace I give to you," Jesus said to his first disciples facing their painful crossroad--their new life after the cross, without his physical presence. "Not as the world gives do I give. Let not your hearts be troubled, neither let them be afraid" (John 14:27)

Crossroad Prayers

Thank you Lord that you want me to be at peace with who I am, and who I am becoming, even when nothing seems to change. You never quit; I won't either. Amen

DAY 68. PEACEMAKERS

James 3:16-18

It must be plain for anyone to see that peace--in all its forms--is essential to "everything needed for this life," and also that the 'war zones'--of all kinds-- are crying out for peace, for God's peace, Jesus' "not as the world gives" peace. So it is also plain that this peace that you and all Jesus' followers are learning must be shared, planted everywhere, in people's lives, and homes, in communities and nations (& also in the church?) Peace belongs in our crossroad prayers for everyday life, and for every workplace. For some peace will be a life work.

Does Jesus have careers in mind when he says, "Blessed/happy are the peacemakers for they shall be called sons (and daughters) of God." (Matthew.5:9) God is the true peacemaker, but he calls his children to be his own hands and feet, his eyes and ears, his voice of peace, carrying with us his peace wherever we live and work. And some of his people invent new kinds of peacemaking work in all kinds of war zones.

Yohannes and Cara, with their family work in East Africa, among other things develop soccer training programs, particularly for at-risk youth, who are vulnerable to the attractions and pressures of violent extremist movements. Their football programs have turned lives around, and turned many to Jesus. Can you see peacemaking at work here? Nothing new about soccer programs, but all kinds of new opportunities in peacemaking.

In Ramallah, West Bank, Amro, a Palestinian (who as a kid in the second intifada threw rocks at Israeli soldiers) and Ohad, an ex-Israeli intelligence officer together run a software company, with a one to one employee ratio of Palestinians and Israelis. They have no political agenda, but are convinced that "good business makes good neighbors." All this even though they are not free of danger from neighbors at home who do not appreciate what they are doing.

Crossroad Prayers

Amro and Ohad want to build trust, because they see that in ten or fifteen years these IT workers will be leading their respective governments, and "We want to be able to talk to each other."

Amro and Ohad may not see themselves as followers of Jesus, but in their business venture, they are true peacemakers.

There are peacemaking careers waiting to be invented right where we live, too. It will never be easy, but what could give greater joy? Peace for your crossroad prayers.

So many war zones in people's lives, homes, communities; help me see peace in those places, and every day to pray peace. Amen

Crossroad Prayers

DAY 69. A GOOD NAME

Romans 15:1-6

We near the end of that long catechism list of "everything needed for this life," with *peace* and *health*. Peace and health--and more--belong together, and in the Hebrew word for peace they are brought together: *Shalom* is the word, and it gathers up the whole of life. Shalom means our total well-being of body and soul and spirit, and all our relationships. Shalom also would include another named 'basic life need, **a good name**. And how we want this one!

What is a good name? Whatever it means, you want your resume somehow to reveal a person with a good name, because you probably know the truth of Proverbs 22:1: "A good name is to be chosen rather than great riches, and favor is better than silver or gold." What is a good name? We have no end of definitions, but could anyone have a better name than in what Paul describes as he writes about God's love at work where the rubber meets the road? "Love is patient and kind; love does not envy or boast; it is not arrogant or rude. It does not insist on its own way; it is not irritable or resentful; it does not rejoice at wrongdoing, but rejoices with the truth. Love bears all things, believes all things, hopes all things, endures all things." (1 Corinthians 13:4-7)
Who could have a better name than one who is learning God's love--or shall we say one who is following Jesus?

So the good name will be seen from day one on the job, and all the days that follow; and it is seen especially as you learn God's heart for coworkers, and so do what you can for their good name. Even in an atmosphere of workplace slander, critical attitudes, or poison rumors, even the simple catechism advice can work: "we are to defend (the neighbour), speak well of him, and explain his actions in the kindest way." (Eighth Commandment, *Luther's Small Catehism*)

That good name, yours and others, is an important part of your crossroad prayers.

Crossroad Prayers

Lord Jesus, I do want a good name; help me care also about my neighbor's good name. Thank you for giving us your Name. Amen

DAY 70. THE CORPORATION
Ephesians 4:11-16

Last on the catechism list of 'daily bread blessings' everyone needs for this life is *true friends and neighbors*. We all know well how important true friends are, and how difficult it can be to find, to make, and keep such friends. To live without true friends is not only a lonely life, but it holds us back from the help, the learning and growth which comes from a friend who is honest and faithful, and speaks truth.

Having friends and neighbors is important for all of life and also for our vocational and work life. Good friends and neighbors are not often a part of our world's economy, so dominated by giant corporations, like Amazon, Google, Facebook, and the like, all of which are basically warring with each other to control as much of the economy as possible, and maybe more than that. Many people, maybe you, from your crossroad search will become part of such corporations.

Corporation comes from the Latin *corpus*, which means body, and the ones we are thinking about are notable bodies of people and complex structures. But Jesus has a corporation too, one quite opposite to the worlds'--his is a living body formed by God's love on earth among his followers. Paul writes: "...speaking the truth in love, we are to grow up in every way into him who is the head, into Christ, from whom the whole body, joined and held together by every joint with which it is equipped, when each part "is working properly, makes the body grow so that it builds itself up in love." (Ephesians 4:15-16)

Maybe this is one of God's definitions of "true friends and neighbors." Yes, quite the opposite of the world's corporate bodies. The body of Christ is imperfect, made up of forgiven sinners like us, but is very much alive and growing and bringing life to many in our wartime world. It happens through countless ministries of his disciples; and it happens also where his members are at work in the world's corporations, bringing life in places and ways only God can see.

Crossroad Prayers

Your crossroad prayers may connect you with one corporation or another, but living constantly within Jesus" corporate body.

Thank you Lord that I am part of your body, wherever you send or assign me. Amen

Crossroad Prayers

DAY 71. BREATH OF LIFE

Matthew 6:5-15

Is it sometimes difficult to pray for Jesus' direction and guidance toward your work life, your vocation? Any prayer can be difficult, since we are all beginners in praying. That is why Jesus carefully teaches us, day by day, how to pray, just as he did with his twelve.
The fifth petition is close to the center of the Our Father, but in truth is the beginning of all prayer: *"Forgive us our sins, as we forgive those who sin against us."* When God turns us around, away from our self-driven life, to ask for his forgiveness, we come to life, because, with his forgiveness, and our trust in his promise, we suddenly have a relationship with him, and this is what it means to be alive. The hymn writer James Montgomery wrote, and sang, "Prayer is the Christian's vital breath, the Christian's vital air." Prayer is our breath of life with God--this prayer and all our other prayers.

But this petition also brings life to our relationships with people, all those we live with, communicate, play and work with. If breathing in our Father's forgiveness is life for us, maybe we can say that breathing out forgiveness for our neighbour, brother, sister, friend, enemy--is life for us and for them--in our relationships with each other.

Jesus makes it plain--the two parts go together, and cannot be separated; they are as close as inhaling and exhaling. "For if you forgive others their trespasses, your heavenly Father will also forgive you, but if you do not forgive others their trespasses, neither will your Father forgive your trespasses." (Verses 14, 15)

The forgiveness prayer belongs with all our prayers, including your crossroad prayers because this prayer breathes life into everything you do. This prayer breathes freedom into us, from the guilt, real or imagined, which can drag us down in so many ways, and many other freedoms as well. So pray on for your call, your career, pray with abandon, pray in his freedom of forgiveness.

Crossroad Prayers

Everybody talks freedom, but few seem to have it. Thank you for teaching me to pray and to receive and learn your freedom. Amen

DAY 72. WARTIME PRAYER

1 Timothy 6:6-12

The next petition in Jesus' basic instruction in praying, which is his basic instruction in living, reminds us again that we live and work and pray --in wartime: "Lead us not into temptation," or as also translated, "Save us from the time of trial." We are tempted every day to take wrong paths, and every temptation is a trial, or a test: am I going to go Jesus' way or am I going to go my way? Jesus teaches us this petition so we can pray our way through, past the bad roads, the bad places and all the injury and damage they bring. Jesus teaches us an everyday lesson in walking past the false advertising of temptation-- and also very much a prayer for your life-work crossroad.

The Psalmist prayed: "Lead me in the paths of your commandments, for I delight in it. Incline my heart to your testimonies, and not to selfish gain." (Psalm 119:35f)

Following Jesus' path--doing what he tells us--is how we learn to delight in his pathway, as in the doing we discover how good and beautiful are his ways, his Father's ways. Our great delight in life is giving up working for selfish gain and instead bringing good things and blessings into the lives of the people around us--bringing God himself, and his world of good gifts. This is a workplace prayer.
The war isn't going to end anytime soon, and the world's temptations will smile at you and call to you every day--especially at your crossroad--to go for more than just 'making a living,' more than your neighbor, more than you need. Paul wrote about it to his young disciple Timothy: "But those who desire to be rich fall into temptation, into a snare, into many senseless and harmful desires that plunge people into ruin and destruction." (v9)

In v.8 Paul gave a much better 'make a living' word: "But if we have food and clothing, with these we will be content." And "Godliness with contentment is great gain." (v6) Selfish gain is always a net loss.

Crossroad Prayers

Godliness is working with Jesus to bring life and shalom to your neighbors, to your world, and every kind of work you could imagine is full of such opportunities.

Lord, I know that desire for 'selfish gain --or other lusts--may not go away, but thank you that I do not have to follow the lies. Amen

DAY 73. WARTIME PRAYER-- CONTINUED
Exodus 3:1-15

Jesus' seventh petition in the "Our Father" family prayer carries right on from the sixth, and it is a fighting prayer; "Deliver us from evil--literally "from the evil" or "the evil one." As this is written we are watching news reports of thousands, millions of people, homes and lives torn apart by hurricanes and floods. Some have died and no one knows what the next day will bring. Some are worried about water being polluted by carcasses and waste, and by industrial toxins. "Acts of God"? And acts of people. One evil leading to another. Wartime evils too are never far away, as we hear stories of bombings of hospitals and school buses filled with children.

Deliver us from the evils! Deliver us from the evil one, who is never far from any of these scenes. Our Lord's Prayer takes us back again to the start of his ministry and his mission, which was to "proclaim the good news to the poor... to proclaim liberty to the captives" and "those who are oppressed" and "sight to the blind." His mission was to deliver many people from many evils and to the "casting out of many demons".

This petition Jesus teaches us has everything to do with your crossroad prayers as his followers, because delivering from evil is what you signed up for!   The world's evils, the enemy's evils are way too much for any of us to understand-- they overwhelm everyone--except Christ Jesus. But once more this prayer shows us his overall purpose for our lives as his disciples--to be part of his liberation work. This means getting into the trenches, the troubles and suffering of your neighbors, with practical knowledge and skills, but also with the wisdom and power and presence of God in your work.

God called Moses to be part of his deliverance of his people from Egyptian slavery. Moses wasn't so sure about it, but the Lord brought him through and used him mightily. You are praying your crossroad prayers because you're not so sure either about your call. But Jesus is leading even as he teaches you how to pray. Most important, this is a

Crossroad Prayers

fighting prayer, for whatever kind of deliverance the people of your world need, and for which God has given you abilities and resources.

The world's evils quickly feel overwhelming; but I think I hear you saying that my small part in your great liberating work is surrounded by your strength and the strength you give me. Amen

DAY 74. WORK AND PRAISE

Matthew 15:29-31

"For the kingdom, the power and the glory are yours, now and forever." AMEN! This praise song, this doxology, isn't included in Matthew's or Luke's account of the Lord's Prayer, but it belongs there as it belongs everywhere Jesus goes. As when he worked signs and wonders in Galilee: "So the crowd wondered, when they saw the mute speaking, the crippled healthy, the lame walking, and the blind seeing. And they glorified the God of Israel." (v.31) Jesus' work and people's praise, always together.

So Jesus teaches us prayer, as children of the Father, and shows us that you really can't come near God without seeing and praising his glory, his might as Creator, life-giver, life-sustainer, and his greatest glory of all-- the coming down of the most high and holy Son of God into our bloody world, in Jesus;, and also coming down into our own days and lives, in the Holy Spirit-- who teaches us everything Jesus does and says. How can we come near God without praise breaking out one way or another?

So learning praise belongs in your crossroad prayers, beginning and end, and everywhere in between, especially also as your coworkers and clients "see your good works and glorify God," because somehow he is in your works. (1 Peter 2:12)

Israel' worship, way back in the days of David's kingdom, and before, called them to bring offerings to the temple--from their flocks and herds, from their grain fields and olive orchards-- their work and their worship always connected.

What does all this praise and worship say to you in your crossroad prayers for work, career, and vocation? How can there be a pathway without it? So finish your prayers for the day with "the kingdom, and the power and the glory are yours, now and forever." And see where He leads you.
Finally comes the AMEN--which means "Yes! So be it!"--your own *amen!*

Crossroad Prayers

Thank you for all your wonderful and impossible words interweaving praise with work; and thank you that with you nothing is impossible. Amen

Crossroad Prayers

DAY 75. JESUS' PRAYER FOR YOU
John 17:1-21

What could be more important in all your crossroads praying than to realize that Jesus himself, as Lord of all his disciples, just before his death on the cross, *prayed for you and your life pathway*? He prayed that night first for his 'eleven:' "They are not of the world, just as I am not of the world..." but "as you sent me in to the world, so I have sent them into the world." (Vv 16, 18)

Then Jesus prays for you, for me, and for all the rest of his disciples: "I do not ask for these only, but also for those who will believe in me through their (his first disciples') word." (v.20) He prays for us--21st century followers-- as he sends us into our 21st century world! Jesus prayed as our High Priest that night before he went to the cross, and, as the writer to the Hebrews also wrote: "he always lives to make intercession" for us.

That he prays for us is dizzying enough in itself --if it "hits home" with us-- but we also can hear **what** Jesus asks for us, and what it means for our lives and our work. Jesus prays, "That they may all be one" which means having a life together as God's own community/family, one in heart and mind, one in desire and will--God's will--and in our work. Jesus prays this powerfully: "*that they may all be one, just as you, Father, are in me, and I in you,* that *they also may be in us...*" One with Jesus, one with the Father; this is way too much for us to grasp, to understand, but it is not too much for us to taste, to experience, to discover, to learn and to live.

Jesus is here praying for us to become true family--like the Father lives in the Son, and the Son in the Father--so we, his own people become true sons and daughters living "in" Jesus and the Father. It means praying along with Jesus for this life together of oneness of heart and mind and will, in our everyday living and working, as children of our Father. Thank you, Lord, that my life is about much more than me; it is about your whole family, our family; show me what this means for my vocation. Amen

Crossroad Prayers

DAY 76. JESUS' ONE BODY
John 17:20-23

You probably appreciate the one who says that he or she is praying for you-- especially if that person is praying along with you in your crossroad search. How do you feel about Jesus' praying for you--2000 years ago and still today --for you who are one of "those who will believe in me through their (his first disciples) word," passed on, generation after generation?

You may not be quite sure what his prayer for our oneness with the Father, the Son, and each other means for your life and vocation, but his meaning may be clearer when we think about why he prayed all this. Jesus asked the Father for our oneness "*So that the world may believe* that *you have sent me... and loved them even as you loved me.*" (vv21, 23) The oneness is really God's love binding his people together, and through us as his family revealing himself to our world.

Somehow everything we do is meant to reveal Jesus, whom the Father sent, because it takes people, live people, together in heart and mind, to do this. Our oneness needs to be lived in our church communities and our family life, and everywhere we go and do what we do, including where we work. In your crossroad search for vocation it is important again to remember that oneness does not mean sameness. The Triune God is one, but the Father is not the same as the Son, nor either is the Spirit the same as the Son or the Father. The three are interdependent and always living, working together as one.

So also you and all your sister and brother disciples are not the same either. Each one is a unique combination of DNA, of qualities, gifts, strengths and weaknesses. Only as we bring and offer our different gifts to Christ, the head of the body, and to each other, can we be one, a live, working body.

So once more we remember that in the church God has given 'apostles, prophets, teachers, miracle workers, healers, helpers, administrators,' and

Crossroad Prayers

countless other gifts and works. So once more you continue your crossroad search, to know and appreciate your own unique gifts and find your unique calling, so that Christ's body may be complete--and one-- that the world may see him and believe.

Lord, it is hard to get out of myself. Help me again today to see you better, and especially all the other beloved members of your body. Amen

Crossroad Prayers

DAY 77. GLORY

John 17:20-26

Everybody loves glory. Every year seems filled with ceremonies and celebrations and awards for achievements in entertainment, sports, arts and sciences; the lights are bright, praises and honors are lavish, and millions watch and take it all in. The human heart loves the glory--even if it is somebody else's. Also in our searching for our place in the world, our career, it is hard not to think sometimes about accomplishments and the glory.

So maybe you, maybe all of us, are somewhat shocked when we hear Jesus praying for **glory**, however different this glory may be. In what he says and does he can be hard to follow! So he prays for us: "The glory that you have given me I have given to them." And why? Again, "that they may be one even as we are one, I in them and you in me, that they may become perfectly one." His glory makes us one. And again he prays "that the world may know that you sent me, and love them even as you have loved me." (vv.22, 23)

Jesus keeps praying that the world will see him in our oneness, but now he prays about **glory**--the glory given Jesus by the Father, and the same glory he gives to us, and not the world's glory. It is true glory he gives, the bright splendor and honor that belongs to God, and the glory that all people long for even if they don't know what it is.

St. Paul says it perfectly: "For God, who said, 'Let light shine out of darkness,' has shone in our hearts to give the light of the knowledge of the glory of God in the face of Jesus Christ." (2 Corinthians 4:6) Here is the glory Jesus prays for you, as his disciple, on the road of your calling. Your own achievements and awards, and maybe your fame will never be enough; such fixations only lead away from our oneness in Christ. But the glory the Father gave to Jesus, and that Jesus gives to you as member of his body is where you will live, becoming one with him and with brothers and sisters, and how he will bring many with you into heaven's family.

Crossroad Prayers

The glory of Jesus is heaven touching earth, even in your workplace.

Your word and your prayers are always way too much for me, which I should expect; and it is wonderful. Lead me today a little more into the light of Jesus' glory. Amen

Crossroad Prayers

DAY 78. THE ROAD FOR YOU

Matthew 28:16-20

What a crossroad time for Jesus' disciples: three years of everyday life together on the road with him, difficult and amazing, and everyday learning, now, suddenly completed! Finis! On that mountain they stood with him--who was dead and now so alive; not a time for remembering or reflecting on days past, but to be shown their discipleship/apostleship road to the future!

Your vocational searching- and- finding time is difficult, full of questions. So was theirs, beyond what I can imagine. But Jesus spelled out what it all meant, as always in plain, simple and impossible words; very clear, and not merely as suggestion or good advice to pray over. His word was command: "All authority in heaven and on earth has been given to me..." (v.18) "Over the top' it was, but unarguable, impossible, yet energizing, even exhilarating? "Go therefore and make disciples of all the nations"--the *ethne* (Greek), the families, the tribes, the clans of all the world.

He sends them out to do what he had been training them for, making disciples, but their road now went way past Galilee or Judea or Samaria; it was to the whole earth. Or, better, to every**one** on earth, or, better yet, to every **community** of people on earth. This was Jesus' **sending** word for these first disciples/apostles. And it is also his sending word for us, for you, in your own workplace call, career, and vocation.

Does it seem too much for you? Or, after working through your readings of scripture, after much prayer and listening, are you beginning to see how his commission fits? Maybe you can see something of your part and your place, and the community of people to whom he may want you to go?

Our world has many kinds of communities--*ethne*, family, tribes, clans, but think also of workplace communities: production, development, commerce, technology, arts, sciences, learning, teaching, organizing, managing, and governing. "Go, therefore… and make disciples of all nations." Jesus first disciples 'got it' and saw their road. Perhaps you also 'get' what he is saying, and have an idea of which workplace community he is trying to show you.

Lord, help me put myself in your disciples' place--that day on the mountain; and to see my own place in that light. Amen

DAY 79. BAPTIZING AND TEACHING
Luke 24:36-49

Jesus' call and command for his disciples was to "Go and make disciples," --and then before you can take a breath, he added "(1) Baptizing them into the name of the Father and of the Son and of the Holy Spirit, (2) teaching them to observe (keep, obey) all that I have commanded you." (Matthew 28:19f) Baptizing must be bringing people into a relationship with the Triune God, and teaching must be passing on everything Jesus gave and taught us.

All this sounds like 'church work'--and it is--and for some a career or vocation in itself, and vital and life-giving. If this is your call, you don't want to miss it! But church work is not mainly about institutions and church buildings and the things that happen there, and all that most people think it is. Church is *ecclesia*, "the called-out ones," --called away from serving the world, and into serving God-in-Christ, as they work in the *world's* institutions and structures, and not-church work communities. Every disciple's work is a small and vital part of the 'baptizing and teaching of Christ.'

Christeen Rico is a young woman who works for a technology company in California's Silicon Valley, who discovered she was "a natural in the marketplace" She plans and launches new retail stores in emerging countries and says that to her "opening each new store is similar in a surprising way to planting a church." Her company's mindset stresses enriching customers' lives through technology, and for her it is like a mission. More than that, she says, "I saw that without Jesus with me in the marketplace, ambition would define me there." She works to weave her faith into her marketplace.

Christeen's presence in her workplace is Jesus' presence, and his baptism and teaching are her base and woven into her life and work. His plan is the same for you, and all disciples, either within the visible church community or---as for most disciples-- outside it.

Crossroad Prayers

Help me Lord to see how discipleship in your word belongs right in the middle of every job, every profession, every workplace--and my workplace. Amen

Crossroad Prayers

DAY 80. FIND THE WAY TOGETHER

Acts 1:12-26

In our crossroad prayers we have much we can learn from Jesus' first disciples and their crossroad prayers. When Peter and John and the others returned to Jerusalem, to that upper room, together with many other followers, what did they do? "All these with one accord were devoting themselves to prayer." (v.14) Jesus had ascended, and even with all he had told them, they surely must have felt in some way like they were on their own, and where do we go from here?

But as they prayed they could not keep from thinking of the one who was not there-- Judas. Peter spoke, and remembered words of scripture: "May his camp become desolate" and "Let another take his place." (v.20) So they prayed that God would show them who "should take his place in this ministry and apostleship." Then "They cast lots for them and lot fell on Matthias, and he was numbered with the eleven apostles."

Most of those in that full house of disciples are not named by Luke. Mary, Jesus' mother was; her place in that body was like no other! Jesus' brother James wasn't named here, but he was soon named overseer of the whole church at Jerusalem. All those gathered had a place, and we can be sure they all prayed for each other.

So also we must know that every one of Jesus' followers, over the centuries, has a place--his own, her own place and work as a member of Jesus' body. We have heard it before and we must hear it again. So also with you: you have your place.

And to find your place you also need brothers and sisters, Jesus followers, who know him and who know you; who can see something in you and in your path that you can't see, and important things that God can show them. You want them to pray like that upper room crowd, to pray your crossroad prayers with you and for you. You don't pray alone.

Crossroad Prayers

Thank you Lord that we can look closely at your first disciples, and do pretty much the same things they did, and by prayer, with scripture, help each other find our way.   Amen

Crossroad Prayers

DAY 81. ALL YOU NEED AND MORE

Acts 2:1-21

Jesus' first disciples' crossroad prayer meeting continued, and "When the day of Pentecost arrived, they were all in one place. And suddenly there came from heaven a sound like a mighty, rushing wind, and it filled the entire house where they were sitting. And divided tongues as of fire appeared to them and rested on each one. And they were all filled with the Holy Spirit and began to speak in other tongues as the Spirit gave them utterance. "

Now they were ready, their preparations were complete. God the Holy Spirit is the one who completes everything for them and for us in our discipleship and on our way. These disciples were all the same followers of Jesus shown in the Gospels, knowing well their own weakness and need, all their questions, and the impossibility of carrying out the work of Jesus' Great Commission;, but with the Holy Spirit--of wind and fire--they were complete! The Spirit is the *parakletos*, God who "comes alongside" as Helper, Comforter, Counselor, so how could they not be complete and "ready for the road," ready for their "mission impossible?"

So also for you, whatever anxiety or uncertainty you may be dealing with as Jesus' follower. God's Holy Spirit has come to you as your Helper, Comforter, Counselor, to help you find your way, your place; and He is all you need.

Remember first of all that the Spirit is the one who helps you pray your crossroad prayers. As Paul reminded the disciples in Rome: "Likewise the Spirit helps us in our weakness. For we do not know what to pray for as we ought, but the Spirit Himself intercedes for us…" (Romans 8:26) The Spirit completes our prayers, makes them what they ought to be, prays with us what we want to pray but don't know how.

Jesus' disciples, about 120 of them we are told, in that upper room, were praying at their crossroad; and heaven broke in and the newborn church broke out. Remember that day as you pray.

Crossroad Prayers

Again Lord help me somehow put myself in that upper room, and remember it all, and to be expectant. Amen

DAY 82. JESUS IN THE WORKPLACE

Acts 2:42-47

Jesus' crossroad prayer as High Priest for us, for you, was and is "that they may be one, just as you, Father, are in me, and I in you, that they also may be in us…" (John 17:21) It's growing up as children of the Father, little brothers and sisters of Jesus, 'walking together' with the Holy Spirit.

Jesus' crossroad prayer for us is also for your relationships with the people you work with and work for, wherever he sends you, "so that the world (your world) may believe that the Father has sent him."

We learn to know others when we begin to understand "where they are coming from." So with the people you work with and work for--and when they see where you are 'coming from"--the family of God.

St. Luke tells us what our family life looked like, in the church's beginning. The first disciples and many new ones "Devoted themselves to the apostles' teaching and the fellowship, to the breaking of bread and the prayers. And awe came upon every soul and many wonders and signs were being done through the apostles. And all who believed were together and had all things in common. And they were selling their possessions and belongings and distributing the proceeds to all as any had need. And day by day attending the temple together and breaking bread in their homes, they received their food with glad and generous hearts, praising God and having favor with all the people. And the Lord added to their numbers day by day those who were being saved." (Acts 2:42-47)

I don't think we can find a better picture of the life of the newborn church *family*. And this is the life all Jesus' followers are learning; and we do have much to learn, and it is not easy, being so contrary to the world's style, but a joy it is! Jesus' family life is not so much about "attending church" as it is about **being** the church --and learning, with all our weaknesses and needs--to **be**, to **become** family.

Crossroad Prayers

Your church home may not look in every way like Luke's description, but this is "where you are coming from" when you go to your workplace. And those around will see it in the way you work and share in your workplace community. And Jesus has opportunity to bless anyone, everyone with glimpses of himself, and even call someone to follow. Jesus in your workplace.

Lord, it takes a lot of learning to live as children of Abba Father, as your family, and to live this way in our world. But you promise to make it happen. Thank you

Crossroad Prayers

DAY 83. YOUR WAR ZONE

Matthew 10:16-31

Lord, where am I going, you pray in your crossroad prayers; where are you sending me? You have asked him about many possibilities, and maybe you have narrowed your field. And you have probably prayed also for some peace on your way.

Jesus does speak peace to us, but he also prepares us for trouble; he reminds us, all his disciples, that our life and work is always in wartime; and you have seen it. Preparing his first disciples for their first mission, he said, "Behold, I am sending you out as sheep in the midst of wolves, so be wise as serpents and as innocent as doves. Beware of men, for they will deliver you over to courts and flog you in the synagogues, and you will be dragged before governors and kings for my sake." (Vv 16-18)

Wherever he sends us is a war zone. The whole world is a war zone because its work, its corporations and institutions are always, for those who run them, about *my* kingdom, not God's, my power, my wealth, my conquests. So Jesus prepares his servants for trouble, for war, for this world as it is. He prayed, "I do not ask that you take them out of the world, but that you keep them from the evil one." (John 17:15)

So also Peter writes, "Beloved, do not be surprised at the fiery trial when it comes upon you to test you, as though something strange were happening to you." (1 Peter 4:12) Of course, those who belong to the world will not--in the long run or in the short run--either escape the war or survive it. But Jesus' workers ("wise as serpents and innocent as doves") labor and fight to set people free. So Peter goes on, "Rejoice insofar as you share Christ's sufferings (living, working in wartime) that you may also rejoice when his glory is revealed." (v.13) And his glory is revealed when people are set free.

The world's war produces only casualties. Jesus by his servants, with his Gospel and his healing brings God's kingdom and sets people free. Which warzone/workplace, is for you?

Crossroad Prayers

Lord, sometimes I can't see or understand the war of our world; help me get past the ruse, the camouflage, and above all see you in everything. Amen

DAY 84. ENEMY DOWN

Ephesians 6:5-20

So you pray, where is my workplace, my war zone?...Where are you sending me, fearless and full of joy? Before he gives you your assignment he wants you to remember --and to learn well--that the people you live and work with *are not* the *enemy,* however difficult and painful the stresses and conflicts may be--not your associates, coworkers, not your clients, customers, patients, students, or your bosses, or supervisors or employers, none are the enemy.

St. Paul spells it out, after writing to servants and masters in Ephesus about workplace problems they may have been having: "We do not wrestle against flesh and blood", not against servants or masters or any human being, "But against the rulers, against the authorities, against the cosmic powers over the present darkness." (vv.12f) Paul also writes about "the spirit that is at work in the sons of disobedience," and adds, "among whom we all once lived in the passions of our flesh."

It might be simpler to say that the devil is the enemy, but we need to recognize the complexities and the pervasiveness of the devil's whole spiritual realm of darkness, which controls and runs most of the world we live and work in; and it is always wartime.

Whatever work/warzone he sends you into, he sends you prepared. To Jesus' "Do not fear" Paul adds, "Take up the whole armor of God, that you may be able to withstand in the evil day... and to stand firm." Jesus gives you "the belt of truth", the 'body armor" of righteousness, with the "shield of faith" and "the helmet of salvation"--and your complete security.

He also gives you your 'offensive' equipment to fight our strange battles: "as shoes for your feet...the readiness given by the gospel of peace... and the sword of the Spirit, which is the word of God." And with all this of course, our primary task of working and fighting: "Praying at all times in the Spirit." Your crossroad prayers are also war room prayers, for our

Crossroad Prayers

Lord's liberation--through us-- of people in our world, including your work world. Jesus entered our world of war "That through death he might destroy the one who has the power of death, that is the devil," the real enemy, and bring liberty to those who are oppressed. Lord, all this feels overwhelming; thank you that it is all in your hands. And so am I. Amen

DAY 85. TEN FIGHTING WORDS

Exodus 20:1-20

In our wartime world we know the enemy--"the prince of this world"--but we may not always see his bondservants, especially those we might call "the gods of this world." Even when they contend with us and we with them we may not recognize them.

Millennia ago, back in that day when God gathered his people, the children of Israel, He prepared them in their lives and their work for war with these "gods." First he said, "I am the Lord your God who brought you out of the land of Egypt, out of the house of slavery. You shall have no other gods." (vv.2, 3) Then he spoke ten brief and loaded words--commandments--words to be spoken again and again, and written on their minds and hearts, and words which they would learn to understand in the keeping, in their doing-- or not doing.

"No other gods" he said, amplified with instructions about using the Name and about the Sabbath; and then he spoke seven warnings against what I am calling the gods of this world: *"Honor your father and your mother...you shall not kill...you shall not commit adultery...you shall not steal...you shall not bear false witness against your neighbor... you shall not covet..."*

It should not be hard to see behind all this the gods of family destruction, the gods of death and violence and of sexual sin, the gods of theft and lying and covetousness, and that they all have a strong presence in our world, and pressures in all human society.

God not only warns and guides us with his Ten Words, but at the same time--if we have eyes to see and ears to hear-- he shows more than ten *workplaces*, crying for the liberation of people harassed by these gods of our world. Think, pray about these ten words and the business and institutional workplaces that come to mind, which are calling for Jesus' servants, workers, like you.

Crossroad Prayers

Lord, open my eyes to recognize these little gods, and to my own gifts and call for working and fighting. Amen

DAY 86. FAMILY WARZONE/WORKPLACE?
Ephesians 5:33-6:4

In your crossroad prayers--as asked before--have thoughts or feelings about family and marriage come up, perhaps in your experience of good family life and marriages, or perhaps the hurts or emptiness of troubled family life? Do these thoughts seem peripheral, or can you hear the Lord calling *you* to invest your life in serving, working to, enrich and strengthen marriages and families in your own world?
The call may come, or become clearer and stronger, when we recognize the gods of this world, especially the family-destroying powers. These powers are at work to prevent or erase the total commitment God planned for husband and wife; they degrade all sexual relationships, and market the sex trade and pornography; these gods downgrade procreation and parents' gifts and blessing of nurturing children. These gods create confusion about being male or female, and what marriage is.

Marriages and families have been troubled throughout human history, but recent decades seem much more oppressive. So do you hear Jesus calling you toward a workplace beyond your own house, a workplace in the middle of our world's marriage and family warzones? As noted before, he sends servants into church ministries, private and public agencies, all work places for listening, for counseling and teaching and prayer, even into ministries waiting to be invented. Jesus sends workers who understand **why** God said, "Honor your father and mother," and "you shall not commit adultery," and "let each one of you love his wife as himself, and let the wife see that she respects her husband," and workers who understand **why** he said "children, obey your parents in the Lord," and "fathers, do not provoke your children to anger, but bring them up in the discipline and instruction of the Lord." (Eph.5:33ff)

Can you hear his call to work and to fight, with the "sword of the Spirit, the word of God," to help bring marriages, families, parents and children into his freedom? This is his life-call for us all, and for some his vocational workplace.

Crossroad Prayers

Thank you for my family life and experience and what you are teaching me; thank you for all that is to come. Amen

Crossroad Prayers

DAY 87. LIFE IN THE SHADOW OF DEATH

Psalm 23

Praying your crossroad prayers you realize that any workplace, any job or profession will be in a warzone, and you also know that you want to work and fight alongside your Lord, and never be victimized by the worlds' gods. God said it to his people Israel, camping together in the Sinai wilderness, "You shall not kill." Their world too was harassed by the 'gods of death,' and many temptations.

In our 21st century we see these gods at work in territorial and terrorist wars, bombing of homes and hospitals, and in the famines that wars create. We see them in our western society in a surge of suicides, in a push for euthanasia, in the destroying of the unborn, and of infants. We see it in profitable drug industries, legal and illegal, and in gangs and their street markets. What about video gaming?

Again, Jesus sends disciples/workers into all death zones, on-the-street workers, police, EMT workers, military, aid workers, medical and drug/addiction workers, pregnancy counselors, hospice teams and legislators. Has he said anything to you in your prayers about these war zones, and the many who are longing, crying out for life?
David wrote it: "Even though I walk through the valley of the shadow of death… I will fear no evil, for you are with me, your rod and your staff, they comfort me." Jesus sends his disciples out, to walk with people in that valley, to *be* his own presence. And as Hebrews (2:14) says, Jesus shared our lives "that through death he might destroy the one who has the power of death, that is, the devil, and deliver all those who through fear of death were subject to lifelong slavery.."

Our life as disciples means being part of his *out-of-death-into-life mission;* maybe it is also in some way your life work, your vocation, your call.

Sometimes Lord I can feel how deep and dark is the valley of the shadow of death; thank you for being there, and help me to 'be there' for somebody.   Amen

DAY 88. GOD'S ECONOMY

Psalm 145:13-21

One more workplace/warzone for your crossroad prayers, and it covers the whole world, and in particular the world's economy--the whole multiform world of business and commerce, of making money, making a living, and as much more than a living as you can get away with.

God warned his people in the wilderness against the 'money gods' when he said "You shall not steal," and "You shall not covet." And we know that fight within our own hearts with the gods of desire, of wants that become needs, and of the greed that can take over one's life. And we see the war in the huge corporations, working, fighting to control the market, or to wipe out the competition. These gods seem to rule the world. Can we even see these gods in the lottery kiosks, a kind of 'prayer place,' money prayers offered to the 'gods of the odds'? The world's economy is the economy of taking, grasping, accumulating everything the money gods offer. It is dismal, it doesn't work--and its days are numbered. It is important to remember John's Revelation seeing the end: "Fallen, fallen is Babylon the great...and the merchants of the earth...who gained wealth from her...will stand far off...weeping and mourning aloud...in a single hour all this wealth has been laid waste." (from Revelation 18)

Jesus, always the revolutionary, calls us, and anyone who will listen, into his *Father's Economy,* the economy of the One who *gives* everything, life and breath, food and clothing, everything from his hand--all free, and for everyone on earth, those who love him and those who hate him. His is the *economy of giving.* Paul tells about it: "In all things I have shown you that by working hard in this way we must help the weak and remember the words of the Lord Jesus, how he himself said, 'it is more blessed to give than to receive" (Acts 20:35) Jesus also taught us the Father's economy when he said, "Give, and it will be given to you, good measure, pressed down, shaken together, running over will be put into your lap. For the measure you use it will be measured back to you." (Luke 6:38) Jesus places disciples into businesses that work to give, to serve, to provide what people need, good products, good services, workers who refuse to steal anything. He sends his servants to work his give-economy right in the middle of the world's take-economy.

In recent years he has been sending disciples out to develop what is called "business as mission," working often in lowest-income communities around the world, helping women and men to establish many small businesses, providing needed products and services, working in and with God's promises for neighbors.

In your prayers at your crossroad talk with him about his *giving economy* and the exciting business opportunities that might be waiting.

Lord, I forget easily that everything we have is a gift from your hand. Show me what I need to learn today about your giving lifestyle. Amen

DAY 89. LIFE WORD
Nehemiah 4

Your crossroad prayers with these scripture readings have probably taken you to places you did not expect to go. Seeing our world as a war zone may have been unexpected, and also seeing your life work/job/career as an assignment to a war zone. Jesus on his assignment knew from day one what he was getting into and you can remember his wilderness war zone confrontation with the enemy.

Jesus also knew well his weapon, and that this weapon was all he needed: "It is written!" His weapon--and his working tool--was the "sword of the Spirit, the word of God." This was his weapon in the wilderness and his tool for the ministry of his Father's word of life and healing. And this is the same word he gave his first followers when he sent them out: "Proclaim as you go, saying, 'The kingdom of heaven is at hand.' Heal the sick, raise the dead, cleanse lepers, cast out demons." (Matthew 10:7f)

He gives you the same word as he sends you out to labor and to fight. And actually you labor is your fight, and your fight is your labor, and all by the word of God.

A well-known 20th century trial lawyer once said: "Since the dedication of my life and practice to the Holy Spirit, (another factor entered his work)...at all times I try to listen to the promptings, leadings, guidance of the Spirit of Truth. "While counseling, I have been counseled; while arguing I have been informed; while cross examining, I have been instructed. As long as I have been able to listen, to be aware, I have been very sure that another Presence is there--and that Presence will guide, if listened to." (*Prayer in Action,* by Helen Smith Shoemaker)
This was one disciple/lawyer speaking of his everyday work.

Whatever your work will be as Jesus' disciple, this "living and active *word* of God" (Hebrews 4:12) and the *Holy Spirit* will be in it, bringing life, beyond what you can see, to your workplace neighbors, friends, strangers, enemies, brothers and sisters. Whatever your work.

Crossroad Prayers

Help me see, Lord, your word and Spirit always in the middle of my work, my job my career; and that my work is your work, and you overcome the enemy, and bring life out of death. Amen

DAY 90. WEAPONS OR TOOLS
Romans 12:9-21

How often have you heard it--or said it yourself--"I want to make a difference-- I want *my life* to make a difference?" When you're looking for a job, or a career path, it is sometimes hard to stand far enough back to be able to ask such questions. On the other hand, thinking about our world as both workplace and war zone must make you think about them.

The workplaces and war zones suddenly come very close to each other when we hear Isaiah's word about "the last days" and the coming of God's kingdom: *"They shall beat their swords into plowshares, and their spears into pruning hooks."* (Isaiah 2:4) (and they shall *"not learn war anymore."*)

"Last days" makes us think about our world's end, but also, as the Bible tells us, about Jesus' Messianic day and bringing the kingdom. And in Jesus we also see weapons made over into working tools for life. As humans our words and actions seem to be used mostly as weapons that can kill. In Jesus our words and actions are the working tool for life and peace. Jesus' words and deeds are for your life and your *workplace--* whatever and wherever.

St. Paul in his letter to the churches at Rome shows us our tools, a whole array of word, deeds, and how to use them: "Let love be genuine. Abhor what is evil, hold fast to what is good. Love one another with brotherly affection. Outdo one another in showing honor. Do not be slothful in zeal, be fervent in spirit, serve the Lord. Rejoice in hope, be patient in tribulation, be constant in prayer. Contribute to the needs of the saints and seek to show hospitality."

These are workplace tools and skills, and they turn lives around and into the way of peace. "Bless those who persecute you, bless and do not curse them. Rejoice with those who rejoice, weep with those who weep. Live in harmony with one another. Do not be haughty, but associate with the lowly. Never be wise in your own sight. Repay no one evil for evil, but give thought to what is honorable in the sight of all. If possible, so far as it depends on you, live peaceably with all."

These plowshares and pruning hooks can turn us workers around too, and away from our own natural and harmful attitudes and actions.

Beloved, never avenge yourselves, but leave it to the wrath of God, for it is written, 'Vengeance is mine, I will repay, says the Lord.' To the contrary, 'If your enemy is hungry, feed him; if he is thirsty, give him something to drink, for by so doing you will heap burning coals on his head.' Do not be overcome by evil, but overcome evil with good." (Romans 12:9-21)

Disciples who are learning to use the Lord's working tools wherever they are sent make way more than a "difference" because God himself is working life in and through them. Through you.

Thank you Lord Jesus for coming to us, and for coming into the middle of our warring world, to work your peace. Thank you for calling me to be part of it. Thank you for your promise, "I will instruct you and teach you in the way you should go." Tell me what to do and I will do it.
Amen and amen

Crossroad Prayers

ACKNOWLEDGEMENTS

These reflections and prayers about what Jesus' call to follow means for vocation--especially for young people at their graduation crossroad--have been pushing, pulling me, trying to break out into print for several years. It seems to me that Jesus gives words, good and important words, to all his followers, day by day, on our way, words to be spoken, prayed, written, published, and sung. Here are some of mine, added to the flow, certainly imperfect and incomplete, yet still, I believe, truly his, as with the words he gives all his followers.

Thanksgiving is always the last word. And I thank God for the people, the family around me who have helped make it happen, more than they know. First, for Bev, my wonderful wife, constant, encourager, insightful, --and proofreader; for our Wednesday afternoon "little flock,' constant in prayer and in presence; for Jan and Grant, listeners, reflecting, with discernment and insight; for Ron Dart, knowing the way, friend and steady encourager, occasional prodder; for Wayne Northey, new friend, also knowing the way, and putting these words into publishable form. I am thankful also for Abbé/pastor Michel Quoist and his *Prayers of life,* which shaped the prayers concluding each days reading.

"Rejoice always, pray without ceasing, give thanks in all circumstances, for this is the will of God in Christ Jesus for you." (1 Thessalonians 5:16ff)

ABOUT THE AUTHOR

The author, Robert Randoy, has been praying graduation/crossroad prayers since his own high school graduation, and with increasing focus on the call to discipleship at subsequent graduations: BA, MDiv, STM. The crossroad prayers continued as children and grandchildren reached their graduations, and in serving as pastor and teacher of young people in congregations in Oregon, Washington and Alberta, Canada. Much prayer also for young men and women graduates-- very much at their crossroads-- while serving on the faculty of the Canadian Lutheran Bible Institute in Alberta. He has also published a book, *Walk With Me, Little Flock,* about discipleship as community, and has published prayer letters for Calgary area Lutheran churches and for World Mission Prayer League-Canada.

Made in the USA
Middletown, DE
12 February 2019